Discover

PHYSICAL GEOGRAPHY

KEITH GRIMWADE

Head of Geography at Hinchingbrooke School, Huntingdon

Hodder & Stoughton

LONDON SYDNEY AUCKLAND

INTRODUCTION

This book covers the themes you need to study for the physical geography part of your GCSE syllabus. However, it is important to realise that physical and human geography are closely related – the "physical earth" is our "human home". You will be reminded of this throughout the book and particularly in the final section which deals with Environmental Issues.

The Enquiries are a very important part of this book because they will help you to arrive at your own conclusions. You will be asked to record information in different ways including maps and diagrams.

Ideas for your own fieldwork projects are included. Please be safe – always work with a partner and if you are surveying a stream, for example, it is best if there are at least three of you so that one person can stay on the bank in case of difficulties. Let your parents know where you are going.

I hope that this book, together with its companion volume Discover Human Geography, will make the world – its scenery, weather and climate, environments and people – more interesting and more alive.

Discover Geography!

Keith Grimwade

ACKNOWLEDGEMENTS

The author would like to thank Simon Bellamy for his helpful comments on the typescript; the Geography Department and pupils at Hinchingbrooke School for trying things out and making many constructive criticisms; and Hattie for posting, proof reading and the index.

Fig. Nos: 8 Ted Harvey; 13 (iv) Michael Black; 13 (vi) and (viii), 109 (ii), 135, 150 (iii), 183 (ii), 242, 266 (ii) and (v) David Jones; 25, 52, Nick Britton and Suzy Skevington; 30 USGS Photo Library, Denver, Co; 44 John Walmsley; 84 Reuters; 102, 175 and 178 Hunting Aerofilms; 115 British Antarctic Survey; 132 Scottish Tourist Board; 138, 149 and 182 British Geological Survey; 144 and 147 G.S.F.

Picture Library; 152 and 153 BP International Limited; 155 John Curtis in Weather, Rocks & Landforms published by Century; 196 NAAS Picture Library; 218 and 225 Michael H. Black; 229 Crown; 235 (i) Evening Echo (Southend and Basildon); 235 (ii) The Guardian; 266 (i) and (iii) Robert Harding Picture Ltd; 267 Peter Hildrew and Susan Tirbutt; 271 and 275 Panos; 277 OXFAM; 105 NASA.

Every effort has been made to trace and acknowledge correctly all copyright holders but if any have been overlooked the publishers will be pleased to make the necessary arrangements at the first opportunity.

© Keith Grimwade 1990

First published in Great Britain 1990
Impression number   10 9 8 7 6 5
Year   1998 1997 1996 1995 1994 1993

British Library Cataloguing in Publication Data
Grimwade, Keith
  Discover physical geography.
  1 Physical geography
  I. Title
  910′.02

ISBN 0 340 42918 6

Typeset in Linotron Zapf by Tradespools Ltd.
Illustrated by Ian Foulis and Associates, Saltash, Cornwall.

Printed in Hong Kong for Hodder and Stoughton Educational, a division of Hodder and Stoughton Ltd, Mill Road, Dunton Green, Sevenoaks, Kent by Colorcraft Ltd.

THE EARTH page 4

WEATHERING page 22

RIVERS page 32

ICE page 52

THE SEA page 68

DESERTS page 80

ROCKS AND SCENERY page 88

WEATHER AND CLIMATE page 96

ENVIRONMENTAL ISSUES page 120

Index page 127

THE EARTH

What is the earth like inside?

We cannot explore the inside of the earth for ourselves. The deepest drill has barely punctured the surface. However, we do have some indirect evidence.

- We can study material coming out from inside the earth through volcanoes.
- When earthquake waves pass from one type of rock to another they change speed and direction. These changes can be measured and they can be used to build up a picture of the earth's different layers.
- The earth's density has been calculated. Rocks at the surface are of below average density. This tells us that rocks below the surface must be of above average density.

Fig 1 Journey to the centre of the earth

ENQUIRY

1 Draw a series of circles one inside the other. The outer circle should have a radius of 64 mm; the next circle in should have a radius of 63 mm; the next a radius of 34 mm; and the smallest a radius of 14 mm. This gives you a diagram of the earth's main layers at a scale of 1 mm = 100 km.

2 Add the following labels to your diagram. They are in the correct order starting with the outer layer.
– crust (solid rock)
– mantle (heavy, thick, molten rock)
– outer core (hot, liquid iron)
– inner core (hot, solid iron)
3 Add a title and the scale to your diagram.

THE EARTH

What is the crust made of?

The average thickness of the earth's crust is 40 km. This is thinner than the diagram in the previous Enquiry suggests. Stick a postage stamp on a football and you will get some idea of its relative thickness! The many different types of rock which make up the crust are put into three groups or "families" – igneous, metamorphic and sedimentary. Their relative importance is shown in Fig 2.

Igneous Rocks

These are formed when hot, molten rock (known as magma) cools down and solidifies. Igneous rocks vary according to the size of their crystals and the minerals they contain.

Basalt is an extrusive igneous rock. This means that it has formed from magma which has flowed out onto the earth's crust as lava. As a result, it cools down very quickly and crystals do not have time to form. Its main minerals are dark coloured and it often appears black in hand specimen (Fig 3).

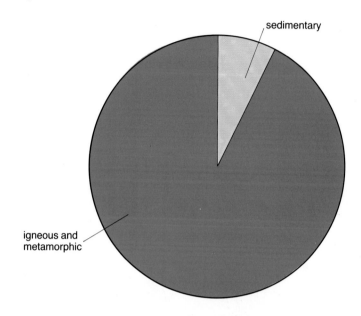

Fig 2 Rocks of the earth's crust

sedimentary

igneous and metamorphic

Fig 3 Hand specimen of basalt

Fig 4 Granite

Granite is an intrusive igneous rock. This means that it has formed from magma which has cooled down inside the earth's crust. As a result, it cools down very slowly and crystals have plenty of time to form. The minerals these crystals are composed of give the granite its colour. In Fig 4 the grey crystals are quartz, the black crystals are

mica and the cream or pink crystals are feldspar.

Basalt often forms volcanoes. Granite forms huge masses deep in the crust called batholiths. If magma pushes its way to the surface *across* layers of sedimentary rock it is called a dyke. If it pushes its way *between* layers of sedimentary rock it is called a sill.

Sedimentary Rocks

There are three main types of sedimentary rock.

- **Clastic** sedimentaries are composed of fragments of other rocks.
- **Organic** sedimentaries are composed of the remains of plants and animals.
- **Chemical** sedimentaries result from the precipitation of chemicals.

Sandstone is a clastic sedimentary rock (Fig 5). The grains of sand are usually deposited in the sea by rivers, although they can be deposited on the land by wind. Chemicals in the water cement the grains together.

Shelly limestone is an organic sedimentary rock (Fig 6). It forms when the shells and skeletons of sea creatures pile up and become cemented together. This rock is rich in calcium carbonate ($CaCO_3$).

Fig 5 Sandstone

Oolitic limestone involves chemical precipitation (Fig 7). It is composed of small spheres of $CaCO_3$ which have been cemented together. The spheres themselves form when a speck of sand or a tiny fragment of shell is rolled backwards and forwards by gentle currents in water rich in $CaCO_3$. The $CaCO_3$ builds up in layers like a snowball.

As the layers of sedimentary rock build up the bottom ones are compressed. Each layer of rock is known as a bed and the lines separating it from the bed below and the bed above are known as bedding planes. Together, the layers are known as strata (Fig 8). A crack in a bed of rock is known as a joint.

Fig 6 Shelly limestone

Fig 7 Oolitic limestone

Fig 8 Layers of sedimentary rock

Metamorphic Rocks

These are igneous or sedimentary rocks which have been changed by tremendous heat and/or pressure. Usually, all traces of the original rock are destroyed.

Marble (Fig 9) is metamorphosed limestone. It forms when limestone is heated to great temperatures, perhaps by a granite intrusion. The zone of heated rock is known as the metamorphic aureole.

Slate (Fig 10) is metamorphosed mudstone, a sedimentary rock made up of fine particles of clay. It forms when mudstone is put under great pressure, perhaps because of earth movements. The minerals in the mudstone are squeezed together and form lines known as cleavage planes. Although slate is a hard rock it splits easily along these cleavage planes.

Fig 9   Marble

Fig 10   Slate

NAME	FAMILY	COLOUR	GENERAL APPEARANCE e.g. crystals? shell fragments?	FORMATION
basalt				
		speckled – white, cream, black		
				grains of sand cemented together
shelly limestone				
			made up of small spheres	
				limestone changed by great heat
slate				

Fig 11   Rock table

ENQUIRY

1 Copy and complete the table in Fig 11.
2 Make a sketch of Fig 8. Label onto it two bedding planes, a bed of rock and any joint that you can see. Give your sketch the title "Sedimentary strata".
3 Copy Fig 12. Label onto it the following terms in their correct place – magma, sill, aureole, lava, batholith, dyke. Then, in your exercise book or file, explain what each of these terms means.

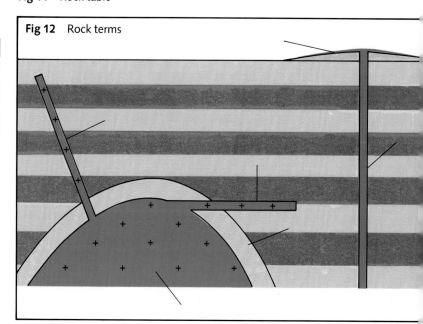
Fig 12   Rock terms

The Economic Uses of Rocks

ENQUIRY

1 We have always made use of the rocks around us. Make a list of the uses shown in Fig 13 and match these with the correct rock from the following list – marble, coal, slate, chalk, granite, limestone, clay. Add to your list any other rocks and the use(s) to which they are put that you know of.

Fig 13 Making use of rocks

Why does the crust keep moving around?

Since the 17th century the possibility that at some time in the past the continents were joined together has been discussed. However, this idea was not taken seriously until 1912 when Alfred Wegener, a German geologist, published his book "The Origin of the Continents". The evidence for what is now known as the theory of continental drift is outlined in Fig 14.

At first many scientists disagreed with Wegener but it is now widely accepted that between about 350 and 200 million years ago today's continents were joined together to form a single "super continent" known as Pangaea. About 200 million years ago Pangaea began breaking up and since then the continents have been drifting apart.

ENQUIRY

1 Which piece of evidence for continental drift do you find most convincing? Why?

2 Trace the outlines of the continents in Fig 15 onto a sheet of plain paper. Cut them out and stick them together in your exercise book or file by lining up the coloured strips – blue with blue, green with green etc. This gives you the shape of Pangaea. Add a suitable title and write a brief explanatory account.

Evidence	Conclusion
● It looks as if the continents fit together like the pieces of a jigsaw puzzle, particularly South America and Africa.	● At some time in the past they were joined together.
● There is evidence of an ice age 280 million years ago in parts of South America, Africa, India, Australia, and Antarctica.	● At this time these continents were joined together and were affected by the same ice age.
● Fossils of a small fresh to brackish water reptile known as Mesosaurus have been found in rocks of the same age in South America and Africa but nowhere else.	● Mesosaurus could not have survived an ocean crossing in salt water so at this time South America and Africa must have been joined together.
● The mountains of North America, Greenland, Scotland and Scandinavia are of the same age and have the same directional trend.	● They were formed when these regions were part of the same land mass.
● Some rocks record the earth's magnetism. Rocks of the same age in different continents show different magnetic trends.	● Rocks of the same age record the same magnetic trend. If, now, these trends disagree the only possible explanation is that the continents they are part of have drifted in different directions.

Fig 14 Evidence for continental drift

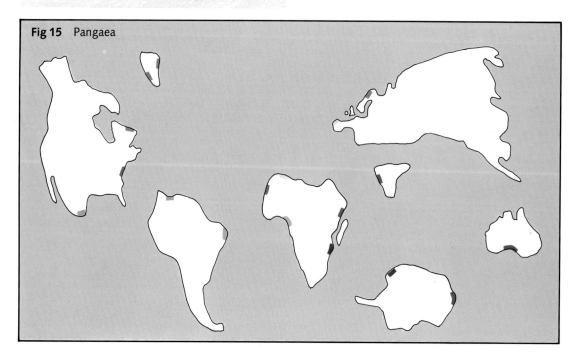

Fig 15 Pangaea

In the late 1950s and early 1960s new evidence about the structure of the earth was discovered from surveys of the ocean floor. It became clear that the earth's crust is not a continuous layer of solid rock. Rather, it is split into a number of pieces by deep cracks. Each of these pieces is known as a "plate" (Fig 16).

In some places these plates are moving towards each other. When this happens the denser plate moves under the less dense plate and is destroyed (= a destructive plate margin). In other places the plates are moving away from each other and magma is rising to fill in the gap (= a constructive plate margin). The third possibility is that the plates are simply moving alongside each other (= a conservative plate margin).

It also became clear that the continents are passengers on these plates. As the plates move the continents have to move with them. So, the theory of "plate tectonics" fits in with the theory of continental drift.

However, why do the plates themselves move? The most widely accepted theory is that this is the result of giant convection currents in the mantle dragging the plates with them (Fig 17).

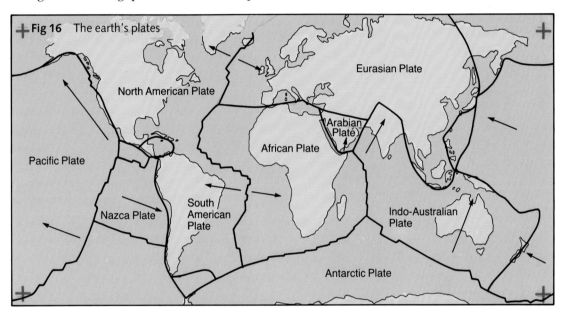

Fig 16 The earth's plates

North American Plate

Eurasian Plate

Pacific Plate

Arabian Plate

African Plate

Nazca Plate

South American Plate

Indo-Australian Plate

Antarctic Plate

ENQUIRY

1 Mark onto an outline map of the world the details shown in Fig 16. Label an example of each of the three types of plate boundary.
2 Write a paragraph to explain the convection current theory of plate movement.

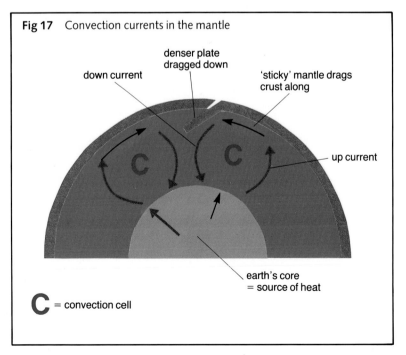

Fig 17 Convection currents in the mantle

denser plate dragged down

down current

'sticky' mantle drags crust along

up current

C

C

earth's core = source of heat

C = convection cell

What happens as the crust moves around?

1 Mark onto a piece of tracing paper the distribution of volcanoes shown in Fig 18. Place your tracing paper over Fig 16 which is drawn at the same scale. The blue crosses will help you to line up the tracing paper correctly. What is the relationship between plate boundaries and volcanoes? Name one place which is an exception to the general pattern. Name the famous volcanoes labelled 1–5.

2 What is the relationship between plate boundaries and the distribution of earthquakes (Fig 19)?
3 What type of plate boundary (constructive, destructive or conservative) are the earth's most recent mountain chains associated with (Fig 20)? Name the mountain chains labelled 6–10.
4 Explain why the U.K. is free from volcanic eruptions and major earthquakes.

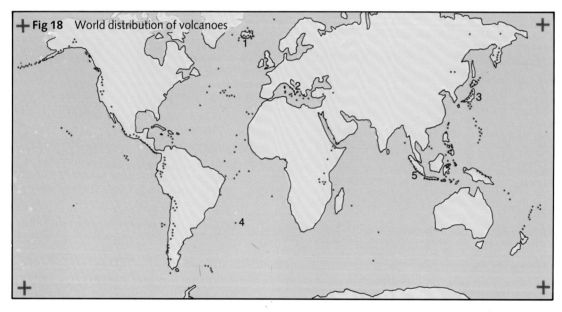

Fig 18 World distribution of volcanoes

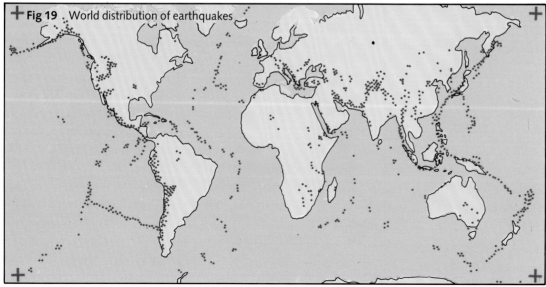

Fig 19 World distribution of earthquakes

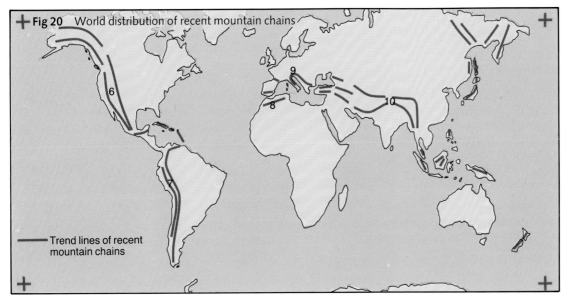

Fig 20 World distribution of recent mountain chains

—— Trend lines of recent mountain chains

Constructive Plate Boundaries

At constructive plate boundaries the earth's plates are moving apart and new material is being added to the crust. Pangaea broke up along a series of constructive plate boundaries. As the continents pulled away from these boundaries the oceans formed and as a result most constructive plate boundaries are found under the sea. The ocean ridges which are shown on maps of world relief in most atlases mark these boundaries.

As the plates pull apart cracks, known as faults, form in the crust. Magma rises to the surface along these faults. It plugs the gap and may add new material to the sea-floor or it may erupt to form a volcano. An example of a volcano associated with a constructive plate boundary is Surtsey which rose out of the sea 100 km south of Iceland in 1963 (Fig 21).

There are two main types of lava – **acid** and **basic**. Acid lava is thicker than basic lava and it flows slowly. This produces volcanoes with steep slopes (see pages 15 to 16). Basic lava flows quickly and produces volcanoes with gentle slopes, known as "shield volcanoes"

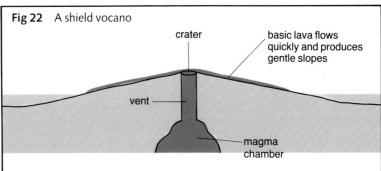

Fig 22 A shield vocano

crater

basic lava flows quickly and produces gentle slopes

vent

magma chamber

(Fig 22). Mauna Loa in Hawaii is an example of a shield volcano. It is, in fact, the largest volcano on earth with a diameter of 200 km at its base on the sea floor and a height of 10 km, 4 km of which is above sea level. However, it is important to realise that Mauna Loa is not on a constructive plate boundary but has another explanation (see page 19).

The lava found at constructive plate boundaries tends to be of the basic type. When it wells out onto the sea floor the water cools the outer layer of the lava forming a skin. The hot lava underneath carries on trying to push its way out. The result is a mass of rounded lumps known as "pillow lavas" (Fig 23).

Fig 21 Surtsey

Fig 23
Submarine pillow lavas

If two parallel faults form as the plates pull apart the crust in between slips down. The result is a feature known as a rift valley. An example is the East African Rift System (Figs 24 and 25). 20 million years ago the Arabian plate began pulling away from the African plate (see Fig 16, page 11). This caused lines of weakness to develop in East Africa and the two sides of the Rift System began to move apart. The land in between slipped down to form the valley and lava welled up along the lines of weakness to form a chain of volcanoes.

Fig 25　The Rift Valley in Kenya

It has been suggested that this system marks an early stage in the break-up of Africa. However, this seems unlikely because it has moved apart by only 10 km in the last 20 million years whereas the Red Sea between the Arabian and African plates has moved apart by 320 km over the same period of time.

Of course, rigid pieces of the earth's crust cannot be pulled apart without earthquake activity. All constructive plate margins are associated with earthquake activity. The focus of these earthquakes (the place where the shock waves start) tends to be at a shallow depth in the crust.

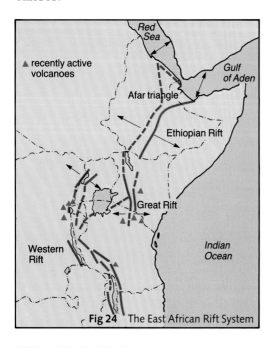

Fig 24　The East African Rift System

see Fig 16, page 11

ENQUIRY

1　Go back to the copy you made of Fig 16, page 11. Find out from an atlas the names of three ocean ridges and add these to your copy.

2　Copy Fig 26. Label onto it the following terms in their correct place:
– pillow lavas
– oceanic crust
– central section has slipped down between two faults forming a rift valley
– volcano
– direction of plate movement
– new material is added to the crust as the plates move apart
– ocean floor.

3　Write a brief account of the East African Rift System. Which countries does it pass through? Can you name any of the volcanoes associated with it?

4　Why do you think earthquakes associated with constructive plate boundaries cause us relatively few problems?

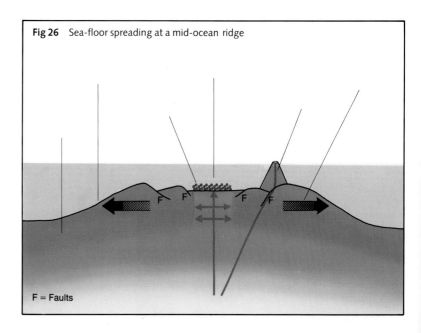

Fig 26　Sea-floor spreading at a mid-ocean ridge

F = Faults

Destructive Plate Boundaries

At destructive plate boundaries the earth's plates are moving together. The denser plate moves under the less dense plate and is swallowed up by the mantle (Fig 27). The place where this happens is known as a subduction zone and it is marked by a deep trench on the ocean floor; an example is the Marianas Trench in the north-west Pacific which is the deepest place on earth.

The temperature increases as the plate moves down into the mantle. At a depth of 100 km the temperature is 1000° C and the plate has already begun to melt. Earthquake evidence suggests that it finally disintegrates at a depth of about 700 km.

The rocks of the earth's crust are less dense than the mantle. As a result the molten rock from the melting plate rises back to the surface. If the plate is moving under a piece of oceanic crust this material erupts as a line of volcanoes which may rise above the surface to form an "island arc"; an example is the Aleutian Islands in the north Pacific. If it moves under a continent the material may form igneous intrusions or it may be able to follow a line of weakness to the surface and erupt as a volcano.

The lava found at destructive plate boundaries tends to be of the acid type (because it comes from crust which has melted rather than from fresh material immediately under the crust). As has been mentioned, acid lava is thicker than basic lava and it flows at a slower rate. This produces volcanoes with steep slopes, known as "acid cones", such as Ngauruhoe in North Island, New Zealand (Fig 28).

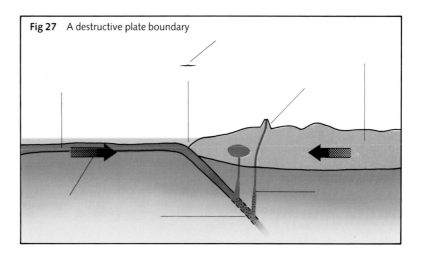

Fig 27   A destructive plate boundary

Fig 28   Ngauruhoe

ENQUIRY

1   Copy Fig 27. Label onto it the following terms in their correct place:
– igneous intrusion
– melting plate
– direction of plate movement
– subduction zone
– acid cone
– ocean trench
– less dense material rises to surface
– oceanic crust
– continental crust.
2   Go back again to the copy you made of Fig 26, page 14. Use an atlas to help you work out the plate movements involved in the formation of the Marianas Trench, the Aleutian Islands, and Ngauruhoe. Note this information and mark these places onto your map (the centre of North Island, New Zealand, will do as an approximate location of Ngauruhoe). What is the maximum depth of the Marianas Trench?
3   Why are destructive plate margins associated with acid rather than basic lava?

Many of the volcanoes found at destructive plate boundaries are "composite cones" which means that they are made up of layers of lava and ash, one on top of the other (Fig 29).

After an eruption the thick acid lava cools and forms a hard plug of rock in the vent of the volcano. Pressure from gas and magma builds up until it is great enough to blast the plug out of the vent. The plug is shattered by the explosion and the fragments of rock settle as a layer of ash. With the plug out of the way the lava flows freely and forms a layer on top of the ash. When the eruption has finished the lava hardens to form another plug and the process begins again.

Earthquakes

Shallow, medium and deep-seated earthquakes are associated with destructive plate boundaries. This explains why earthquakes are a constant hazard in places like Japan. The focus of these earthquakes appears to be the upper surface of the descending plate.

Tsunamis

These are tidal waves started by submarine volcanic eruptions and/or earthquakes. Nearly all tsunamis are associated with the destructive plate boundaries of the Pacific Ocean. They very often cause more deaths than the eruptions and/or earthquakes themselves. For example, when Krakatoa

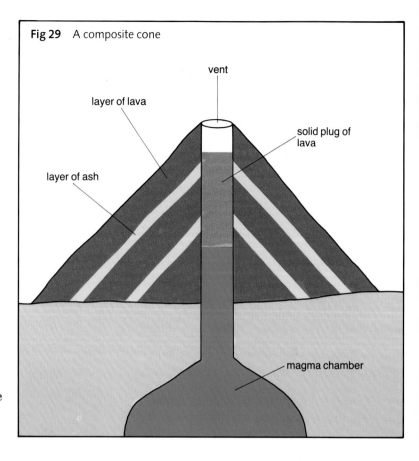

Fig 29　A composite cone

vent

layer of lava

solid plug of lava

layer of ash

magma chamber

erupted in 1883 most of the 36 000 deaths were the result of the tsunamis, up to 35 metres high, which crashed onto the shores of Java and Sumatra. Similarly, tsunamis were responsible for most of the 115 deaths in the Alaskan earthquake in 1964 (Fig 30).

Fig 30
Ships swept ashore by tsunamis during Alaskan earthquake, 1964

Fold Mountains

All the time, sediment is being washed into the seas and oceans by rivers. This builds up on the sea floor as sedimentary rock. These deposits are less dense than the rocks of the oceanic crust or the mantle. As a result, they crumple up like folds in a blanket instead of being dragged down into the mantle along a subduction zone.

If two plates are moving towards each other and one of them has a continent as a passenger these sediments may pile up as a chain of fold mountains along the edge of the continent (Fig 31).

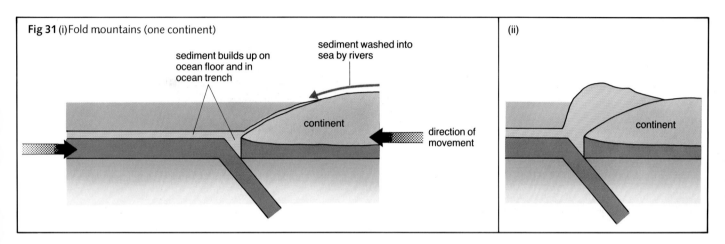

Fig 31 (i) Fold mountains (one continent)

sediment builds up on ocean floor and in ocean trench

sediment washed into sea by rivers

continent

direction of movement

(ii)

continent

If two continents are moving towards each other the sediments are crumpled up between them. Eventually, the continents

themselves may collide and this makes the folding even more intense (Fig 32).

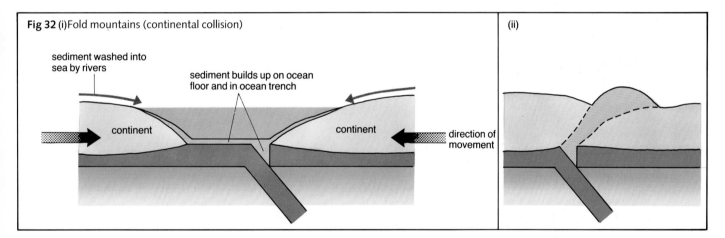

Fig 32 (i) Fold mountains (continental collision)

sediment washed into sea by rivers

sediment builds up on ocean floor and in ocean trench

continent

continent

direction of movement

(ii)

ENQUIRY

1 Draw a diagram of a composite cone volcano. Add detailed labels to explain how this type of volcano forms.

2 Why are deep-seated earthquakes associated with destructive plate boundaries whereas only shallow earthquakes are associated with constructive plate boundaries?

3 What are tsunamis and what are their consequences?

4 Copy Fig 31 (ii) and Fig 32 (ii). Add labels to these diagrams to explain why fold mountains have formed.

5 Compare Fig 16, page 11 with Fig 20, page 13. Name one example of a chain of fold mountains which has formed because of two plates moving towards each other, one carrying a continent. Name one example of a chain of fold mountains which has formed because of a collision between two continents.

Conservative Plate Boundaries

At conservative plate boundaries the earth's plates are moving alongside each other. They are called "conservative" boundaries because, theoretically, material is neither created nor destroyed – one plate simply slides past the other. However, at most of these boundaries some stretching and/or compression takes place and this can result in volcanic activity, mountain building and the formation of rift valleys.

An example of a conservative plate boundary is the San Andreas fault in California (Figs 33 and 34). Here, the Pacific plate and the North American plate are moving past each other at an average speed of 5 cm a year. However, this movement does not happen smoothly. It is easy to imagine why slabs of rock get stuck when they are dragged past each other. The strain builds up to a point and then the rocks jerk apart causing an earthquake.

The San Andreas fault passes through densely populated areas such as Los Angeles and San Francisco. The fault therefore presents a major natural hazard – for example, San Francisco was destroyed by an earthquake in 1906. Since the average movement of the fault is known it is possible to locate places where stress is building up – these are places which have not moved for a number of years. However, although likely areas for an earthquake can be pin-pointed, it is impossible to predict their exact location and timing (Fig 35).

The potential damage of a major earthquake in California is so great that scientists are exploring ways of preventing strain from building up along the line of the fault. One idea is to pump water down the fault in order to lubricate it. Another idea is to use explosions to relieve the strain in a controlled way.

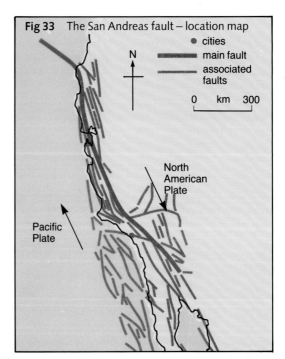

Fig 33   The San Andreas fault – location map
- cities
- main fault
- associated faults

0   km   300

North American Plate

Pacific Plate

Fig 34   The San Andreas fault

ENQUIRY

1   Mark Los Angeles and San Francisco onto a copy of Fig 33. How long will it take for the San Andreas fault to move the distance between these two cities?

2   The map suggests one of the reasons why predicting the location of earthquakes in California is so difficult. What is it?

3   "Pumping water in Los Angeles may stop an earthquake there but start one in San Francisco". Explain this statement.

Fig 35   Earthquake damage – Bay Bridge, San Francisco 1989

Hot Spots

You learnt from the Enquiry on page 12 that not all volcanoes are found at plate boundaries; Mauna Loa in Hawaii has been mentioned as an example of such a volcano (Fig 36). These "exceptions to the rule" seem to be associated with pools of particularly active magma known as "hot spots".

The cause of these hot spots is far from clear. However, it would appear that although the earth's plates are moving the hot spots themselves stay in the same place. This explains the chain of extinct volcanoes running to the north and west of Hawaii (Fig 37).

Types of Fold

A fold is a bend or curve in a bed or rock. Many folds are the result of rocks being crumpled at destructive plate boundaries (see page 17). However, there are other possible causes, e.g. rocks being distorted in an earthquake or by an igneous intrusion.

If the beds or rock are bent down into the shape of a trough, the fold is known as a syncline. If they are bent up into the shape of

Fig 36   An eruption on Mauna Loa, Hawaii

an arch they are known as an anticline. If the top of the anticline is pushed over slightly the structure is known as an overfold but if it is pushed over so much that the limbs of the fold are almost horizontal it is known as a recumbent fold. These different types of fold are shown in Fig 38 (i)–(iv).

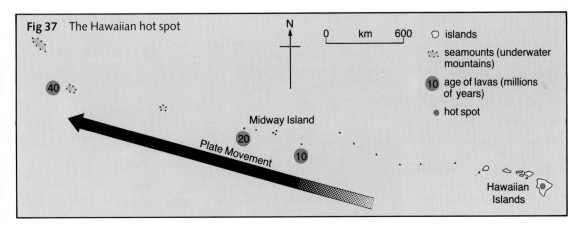

Fig 37   The Hawaiian hot spot

N

0   km   600

○ islands

⋰ seamounts (underwater mountains)

⑩ age of lavas (millions of years)

● hot spot

40

Midway Island

20

10

Plate Movement

Hawaiian Islands

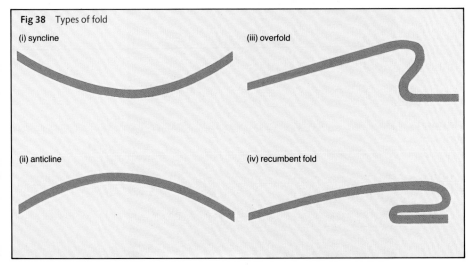

Fig 38   Types of fold

(i) syncline

(iii) overfold

(ii) anticline

(iv) recumbent fold

ENQUIRY

1 Sketch Fig 39. You will find it easier to concentrate on only a few beds of rock rather than trying to show them all. Label two different types of fold. Label any other features you can see such as joints and bedding planes.

Fig 40 Types of fault

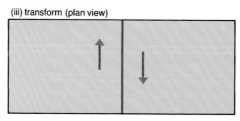

(i) normal (cross section)

fault line — relative downward movement — terminal curvature — relative upward movement

(ii) reverse (cross section)

(iii) transform (plan view)

ENQUIRY

1 What is the difference between a joint (see page 7) and a fault?
2 Sketch Fig 41. Label the type of fault shown. Label any other features you can see such as terminal curvature, joints and bedding planes.
3 What type of faulting do you think is associated with a rift valley and why?

Fig 39 Folding at Stair Hole, Dorset

Types of Fault

A fault is a crack in a rock along which there has been movement. Faults have already been mentioned in connection with constructive plate boundaries where plates are pulling apart (see page 14), although any type of earth movement can cause faulting.

If the rocks are pulled apart one side of the fault has to move downwards; this type of structure is known as a normal fault. If the rocks are pushed together one side of the fault moves upwards to form what is known as a reverse fault. If the rocks simply move alongside each other the structure is known as a transform fault. These different types of fault are shown in Fig 40 (i)–(iii).

As the rocks are dragged against each other along the line of the fault they may be bent slightly. This is a type of folding which is known as terminal curvature.

Fig 41
Faulting at Kimmeridge Bay, Dorset

1   Revise the work done for Section 1.4
Then, copy and complete the Plate
Tectonics Summary Table, Fig 42.

Fig 42   Plate tectonics summary table

	Movement apart, together, alongside?	**Crust** created, destroyed, conserved?	**Volcanoes** yes, no? (if yes, basic or acid cone?)	**Earthquakes** shallow, medium, deep?	**Fold Mountains** yes, no?	**Type of Fault** normal, reverse, transform?	**Rift Valleys?** yes, no?
Constructive Plate Boundary							
Destructive Plate Boundary							
Conservative Plate Boundary							

ROCK SURVEY

The best exposures of rock in this
country are usually found in cliffs on
the coast or in quarries. If you live near
one of these places a rock survey is easy
to organise. However, most rocks are
hidden beneath fields or concrete.
Nevertheless, we use many different
types of rock in our buildings and this
makes a survey of a different kind possible.

Walk through any town or city with
your "geological" eyes open and the
variety of rocks will probably surprise
you! Stone buildings, such as the oolitic
limestone walls of Oxford colleges (Fig
43), are an obvious start-point. Major
buildings are often decorated with
polished marble or granite (Fig 44).
Bricks are made from clay. The colour
of older bricks in particular reflects the
type of clay they were made from (Fig 45).

●   Plan and write an account of a
"geological walk" of about 2 km through
the settlement you live in, or one near
you. It should include a map of the
route with the places where different
types of rock can be found marked onto
it. Describe the rocks carefully. Try to
find out the names of the rocks. This is
not always easy but books in the local
library should provide some answers;
also, the people who live or work in the
buildings may be able to help. Try to
find examples from each of the three
families of rock (see pages 6 to 8).

Fig 43   Oolitic limestone for building

Fig 44   Polished rock for luxury decoration

Fig 45
Bricks made
from Oxford Clay

WEATHERING

Why do rocks break down?

Weathering is the name given to the process by which rocks break down when they are exposed to the earth's atmosphere. In the end all rocks disintegrate because of this process, even the hardest.

Physical Weathering

This is the mechanical breakdown of rocks, usually because of changes in temperature.

Freeze-thaw weathering happens when water gets into a crack in a rock and freezes. As the water turns to ice it expands in volume by about 9%. This exerts a strain on the rock which may be enough to split it. When the ice melts the water trickles into another crack – if it then freezes and turns to ice the process is repeated (Fig 46). This type of weathering is most common in areas where the temperature hovers around freezing point.

Onion-skin weathering (or exfoliation) happens when a rock is repeatedly heated and cooled. This type of weathering is important in the hot deserts where there is a big difference between daytime and night time temperatures. As it is heated the outer layer of the rock expands slightly and as it is cooled it contracts. Continual expansion and contraction exerts a strain on the rock and its surface begins to split away in layers (Fig 47). Moisture getting into the cracks and decomposing the rock would appear to be a very important part of this process (see page 82).

The angular rock fragments which result from physical weathering are known as scree. They can build up to form a scree slope (Fig 48).

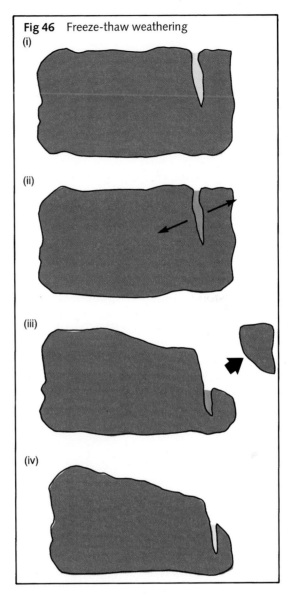

Fig 46 Freeze-thaw weathering

(i)

(ii)

(iii)

(iv)

Fig 47 Onion-skin weathering

Fig 48 Scree slope

WEATHERING

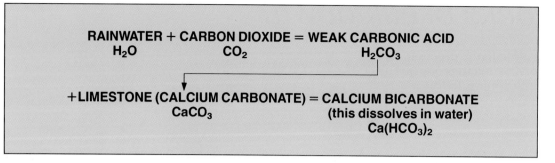

RAINWATER + CARBON DIOXIDE = WEAK CARBONIC ACID
H_2O CO_2 H_2CO_3

+LIMESTONE (CALCIUM CARBONATE) = CALCIUM BICARBONATE
$CaCO_3$ (this dissolves in water)
$Ca(HCO_3)_2$

Fig 49 The chemical weathering of limestone

Chemical Weathering

Chemical weathering is mainly the result of rocks dissolving in rainwater. This happens because as rainwater passes through the atmosphere and the soil it picks up carbon dioxide and becomes a weak carbonic acid.

Carbonic acid reacts with some rocks more than others. Its effect on limestone is dramatic. Fig 49 shows the chemical reaction which takes place – the rock is dissolved completely.

However, the rate at which this reaction takes place is relatively slow. Fig 50 shows a sandstone boulder resting on a pedestal of Carboniferous Limestone at Norber in North Yorkshire. The boulder is impermeable and has protected the limestone underneath it from the rain. The limestone around it has therefore been lowered by the height of the pedestal, 45 centimetres, since the boulder was deposited by an ice sheet about 100 000 years ago.

The effect of weak carbonic acid on granite is shown in Fig 51. Of the three main minerals only feldspar dissolves but this is enough to cause the rock to crumble. The other minerals can then be transported away.

Any undissolved material which is left behind is known as a residual deposit. Laterite soils are an example. These form in the hot, wet, humid climate of the tropics where rapid chemical weathering dissolves most minerals. However, iron and aluminium hydroxides are left behind and these build up to form the characteristic red soils (Fig 52).

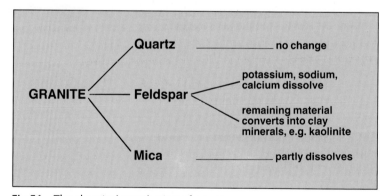

GRANITE

Quartz —————— no change

Feldspar < potassium, sodium, calcium dissolve

remaining material converts into clay minerals, e.g. kaolinite

Mica —————— partly dissolves

Fig 51 The chemical weathering of granite

Fig 50 The Norber Rocks

Fig 52 A laterite soil in Kenya

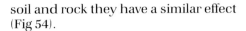

Biological Weathering

This type of weathering involves plants and animals and it is a mixture of physical and chemical processes.

The roots of plants and trees can get into cracks in a rock. As they grow they exert pressure on the rock which can be enough to split it (Fig 53). When animals burrow into soil and rock they have a similar effect (Fig 54).

Decaying vegetation releases organic acids which dissolve rock. Similarly, some animals release acids which attack rock e.g. limpets are a factor in the weathering of rocks on the sea shore.

Fig 53 Roots breaking up soil and rock

Fig 54 Animals burrowing into soil and rock

ENQUIRY

1 Write down a definition of the term "weathering".
2 Copy the diagrams in Fig 46. Add labels to explain freeze-thaw weathering.
3 Make a sketch of Fig 47. Add labels to explain onion-skin weathering.
4 Explain how and why rainwater dissolves limestone. What has been the average rate of weathering of the limestone in the Norber area of North Yorkshire in the last 100 000 years?
5 Copy and complete the table, Fig 55.
6 How do we affect the natural rate of weathering?

Type	Plant Activity		Animal Activity	
	physical	chemical	physical	chemical
Example				

Fig 55 Biological weathering

The Type and Speed of Weathering

The type and speed of weathering varies from place to place. In human terms the process is slow. You have already calculated the rate of weathering of Carboniferous Limestone in North Yorkshire. Another example is that in the last 250 years the oolitic limestone blocks of St Paul's Cathedral in London have weathered by 10 mm. However, in geological terms weathering has enough time to change entire landscapes.

ENQUIRY

1 Copy Fig 56 and complete it by using statements from the following list. You must use all of the statements but because there are only six you should use two of them twice:
– more rapid chemical weathering
– less rapid chemical weathering
– freeze-thaw weathering
– onion-skin weathering
– more rapid weathering
– less rapid weathering

2 What type(s) of weathering would you expect to find in the following regions and why?
– a tropical rain forest
– a hot desert
– the Lake District
– the Arctic region of Scandinavia

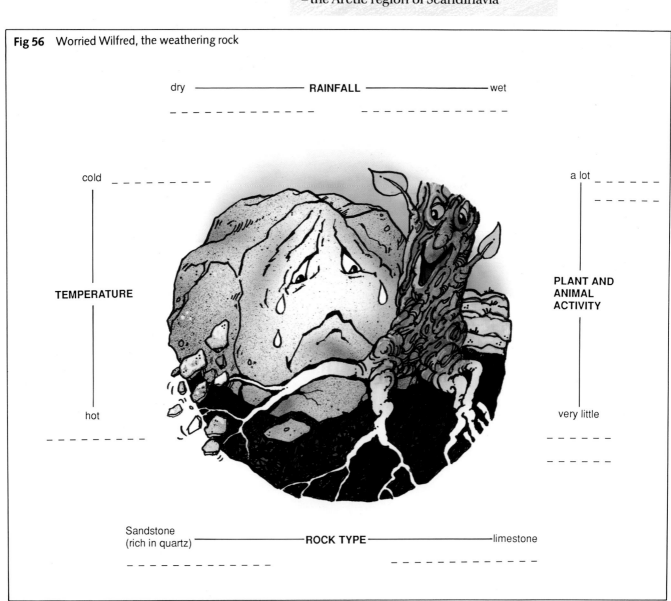

Fig 56   Worried Wilfred, the weathering rock

dry ———————— **RAINFALL** ———————— wet

cold

a lot

TEMPERATURE

PLANT AND ANIMAL ACTIVITY

hot

very little

Sandstone (rich in quartz) ———————— **ROCK TYPE** ———————— limestone

WEATHERING SURVEY

Weathering is not an easy topic for a survey because it is such a slow process and its effects are not always obvious. However, even in a town or city there are things that you could do.

One possibility is a mapping survey. Choose a small area, preferably one which includes old and new buildings. Note on your map any evidence of weathering e.g.

- damage to brickwork (Fig 57) is a sign of physical weathering
- old walls often show signs of damage by plants and animals (Fig 58)
- physical and chemical weathering has often removed the features from statues (Fig 59)

Describe the type of brick or rock. Comment on the degree of damage. It may also be possible to find out the date of the building which will give an idea of the rate of damage.

Another possibility is to study the weathering of gravestones. Make sure you get permission from the people in charge of the cemetery before carrying out such a survey. Many different types of rock are used for gravestones – marble, limestone, sandstone, granite – and you should try to identify these different types of rock first. Then, if you can find two gravestones made from different types of rock but with the same date you can compare the quality of the lettering. This will tell you which type of rock has weathered more quickly. Alternatively, if you can find two gravestones made from the same rock but with different dates you can compare the quality of the lettering and get an indication of the rate of weathering of that type of rock.

Fig 57

Freeze-thaw weathering damaging brickwork

Fig 58

A wall damaged by tree roots

Fig 59

A statue damaged by weathering

Fig 60   Weathered gravestones

What happens to weathered material?

A number of different things can happen to weathered material:

- Much of it breaks down into even smaller fragments forming, in the first instance, a mixture of soil and rock known as regolith. As the rock fragments become even more weathered a layer of proper soil develops. This layer of regolith and/or soil helps the weathering process itself by holding water against the bedrock.
- If the weathered material is on a slope it may move downhill under the influence of gravity. This process is known as mass movement. Three types of mass movement involving weathered material – soil creep, mudflows and rock avalanches – are explained below.
- A great deal of weathered material is transported (moved) by water or wind.

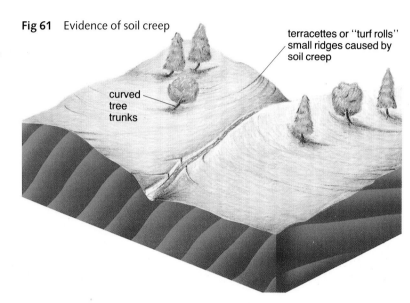

Fig 61   Evidence of soil creep

terracettes or "turf rolls" small ridges caused by soil creep

curved tree trunks

Soil Creep

This is the slow, downhill movement of soil and weathered material. Tilted fences, bulging walls and tree trunks curved at their base are evidence of this process (Fig 61). Soil creep is helped by rainwater and, in particular, by frost and ice (Fig 62). Observed rates of soil creep in this country have been as little as 1 or 2 mm a year.

In cold climates permafrost (permanently frozen soil) covers large areas. The top layer of permafrost often melts in the spring or summer. This can lead to a more rapid type of soil creep as the soil and weathered material slides over the frozen layer below. This process is known as solifluction.

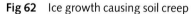

Fig 62   Ice growth causing soil creep

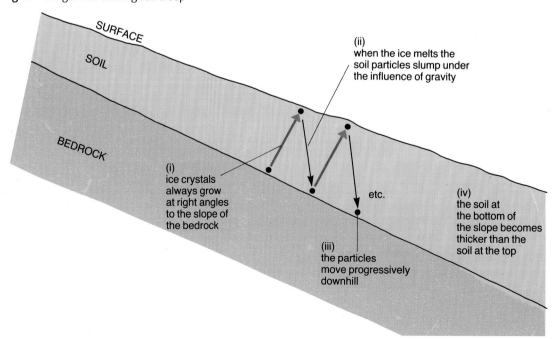

SURFACE

SOIL

BEDROCK

(i) ice crystals always grow at right angles to the slope of the bedrock

(ii) when the ice melts the soil particles slump under the influence of gravity

(iii) the particles move progressively downhill

etc.

(iv) the soil at the bottom of the slope becomes thicker than the soil at the top

Mudflows

Mudflows are a more rapid movement of soil and weathered material. The process involves more water and it is associated with steeper slopes. Fig 63 is of a mudflow at Alum Bay on the Isle of Wight. Soil, weathered material and the fine clays and sands of the cliffs have become saturated and have started to flow across the beach.

In semi-arid regions large masses of fine weathered material often build up on hillslopes because there is very little water to carry it away. When there is rain it tends to fall as a sudden, heavy downpour. The weathered material quickly becomes a soggy mass which flows downhill at a rapid rate. These mudflows are very powerful and are capable of considerable erosion. They continue until they run out of energy on slower, flatter ground (Fig 64).

Fig 63
Mudflow, Alum Bay

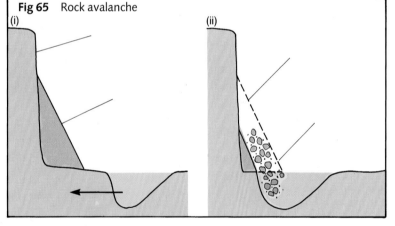

Fig 64
Top of mudflow, California

Rock Avalanches

These are associated with scree slopes. The slow movement of screes is known by the special term "talus-creep". However, if a scree slope is lubricated by heavy rain or melting snow it may move much more rapidly causing a rock avalanche. Another cause of rock avalanches is when a river de-stabilises a scree slope by undercutting it (Fig 65).

Fig 65   Rock avalanche
(i)   (ii)

ENQUIRY

1   Define and/or explain each of the following terms:
– regolith
– mass movement
– transportation
– soil creep
– permafrost
– solifluction
– talus-creep
– mudflows
– rock avalanches
2   Study Fig 62. Explain how and why ice helps the process of soil creep.
3   Add labels to a copy of Fig 65 to explain how and why the river has caused a rock avalanche.
4   Copy the table, Fig 66. Complete it by adding an appropriate comment in each box. Some have already been done for you.

Fig 66   The mass movement of weathered material

	amount of water involved	speed of movement	degree of slope	size of particles
soil creep	some		gentle	
talus-creep		slow		medium and larger rock fragments
mudflows		more rapid		mixed – fine particles and larger rock fragments
rock avalanches	a lot			

What other types of mass movement are there?

The types of mass movement we have looked at so far have involved only soil and weathered material. However, mass movement can also affect the underlying rocks. This type of movement takes place along a definite plane (surface). It is a rapid movement and although the general term landslide is used to describe it, two different types of process can be identified – slides and slumps.

Slides

These happen along a structural plane, such as a bedding plane or joint. They are common where permeable rocks lie on top of impermeable rocks. The bedding plane between the two types of rock becomes wet and slippery and if the permeable rock is unsupported – for example, in a cliff – the pull of gravity causes it to slide (Fig 67).

There are many examples of slides along the Dorset coastline. For example, at Houns-tout Cliff the rocks are dipping gently towards the sea and light coloured blocks of permeable limestone have slipped over dark coloured blocks of impermeable clay (Fig 68).

Slumps

These happen along a curved shear plane. The slumped material tilts backwards along this plane, a movement known as rotational slip (Fig 69). Again, this process takes place because of saturation and the pull of gravity. Slumps are common in clay because it deforms easily when it is wet. However, slumping can also happen when two or more layers of rocks are involved.

Fig 67   Sliding

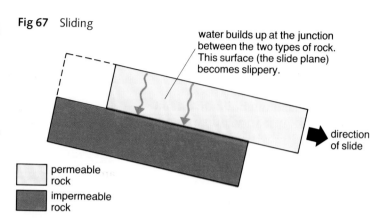

water builds up at the junction between the two types of rock. This surface (the slide plane) becomes slippery.

direction of slide

☐ permeable rock

■ impermeable rock

Fig 68   Houns-tout Cliff

☐ clay

Fig 69   Slumping

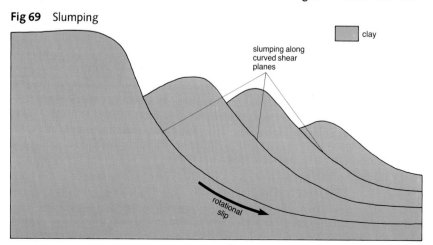

slumping along curved shear planes

rotational slip

Landslides at Folkestone Warren, Kent

At Folkestone Warren there is a 4 km stretch of coastline where 120 metres of permeable chalk lies on top of 45 metres of impermeable Gault Clay. The junction between these two rocks becomes very slippery after heavy rain. Also, the weight of the chalk forces the clay out at the base of the cliff. The combination of these two characteristics results in massive rotational slips.

The first recorded landslide at Folkestone Warren was in 1765. The main Folkestone–Dover railway line runs along this stretch of coastline and in 1915 a major slip derailed a train and closed the railway for 4 years. There were further major slips in 1937 and 1940. In order to reduce the risk of slips drains have been dug into the cliffs and concrete sea defences have been built along the shore. As a result there have been fewer movements in recent years.

In the photograph of Folkestone Warren (Fig 70) you can see, in the background, the steeper profile of the chalk cliffs which have not been affected by landslides. In the foreground is the jumbled mass of slipped material.

There are many examples of landslides causing loss of life and/or property. Some examples are given in Fig 71.

Fig 70   Folkestone Warren

ENQUIRY

1   What are the differences between a slide and a slump?
2   Make a sketch of Fig 70. Add labels to explain why Folkestone Warren has been affected by landslides.
3   Explain why a) drains and b) concrete sea defences are likely to reduce the risk of landslides at Folkestone Warren.
4   Do landslides make slopes steeper or gentler? Explain your answer.
5   In what ways are landslides a) different and b) similar to soil creep? (Comment on their human impact as well as their physical characteristics.)

Location	Date	Description	Human Impact
Vaiont Dam, 100 km north of Venice in Italy	9/10/1963	a giant landslide plunged into the reservoir behind the dam	2 600 deaths, widespread loss of property
Aberfan, South Wales	21/10/1966	a coal tip heap collapsed	147 deaths including 116 children in Pantglas Junior School which was destroyed
Blackgang, Isle of Wight	March 1978	saturation of sands and clays leading to a series of landslips	property losses of £150 000 – cottages, caravans, chalets and part of a holiday camp were affected

Fig 71   Landslides, a natural hazard

RIVERS

What makes up a river system?

River Basins

A river basin is the total area drained by a river and its tributaries. (Tributaries are small streams or rivers joining a main one.) The line separating one river basin from another is known as the watershed. A river basin and watershed have been marked onto Fig 72.

Stream Ordering

River basins can cover thousands of square kilometres and a main river can have many tributaries. Stream ordering is a way of describing a river system so as to make it seem less complicated.

A stream flowing away from its source (the place where it begins) is known as a first order stream. If two first order streams join together the result is a second order stream. If two second order streams join together the result is a third order stream, and so on.

It is important to remember that it is only when two streams of the same order join together that the stream order goes up e.g. if a first order stream joins a second order stream it remains a second order stream.

The place where two streams join together is known as the confluence.

Drainage Density

This is worked out by adding up the length of all the streams in a river basin and dividing by its area. In particular, it is a useful measurement for comparing river basins.

ENQUIRY

1 Make a copy of Fig 72. Show any other river basins you can identify by drawing on their watersheds. Choose one of these river basins and carry out a stream ordering exercise. Calculate its drainage density.
2 How do you think the following factors will affect drainage density – a) rock type (permeable/impermeable); and b) climate (wet/dry)?

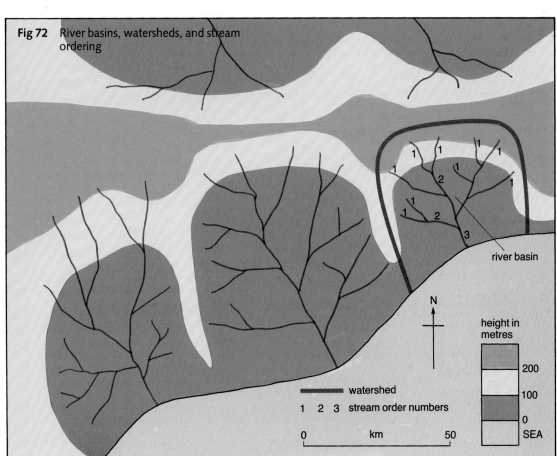

Fig 72 River basins, watersheds, and stream ordering

river basin

N

height in metres

200

100

0

SEA

—— watershed

1 2 3   stream order numbers

0   km   50

Drainage patterns

The patterns made by a river system vary from basin to basin, largely because of differences in rock type and structure. Four main patterns can be identified and these are shown in Fig 73.

A **dendritic** pattern is like the shape of a tree – the main river is the trunk and the tributaries are the branches and twigs. This pattern develops in areas of uniform rock type and structure.

A **trellised** drainage pattern has the tributaries arranged more or less at right angles to each other. This pattern develops in areas where there are alternating bands of hard and soft rock which all dip in the same direction. A river flowing in the direction of dip is known as a consequent river; one flowing at right angles to the dip is known as a subsequent river.

A **radial** drainage pattern has the rivers flowing outwards from a central point. This pattern develops in areas where the rocks form a dome or cone.

A **centripetal** drainage pattern has the rivers flowing inwards to a central point. This pattern develops in areas where the rocks form a basin.

ENQUIRY

1 Draw sketch maps of the river systems listed below. (You will find them on the physical maps in your atlas.) For each river system, state the type of drainage pattern and briefly list the reasons for its development.
– the River Amazon (Brazil)
– the River Thames between Slough and Cirencester
– the rivers of the Lake District
– the rivers of the Aral Sea (U.S.S.R.)

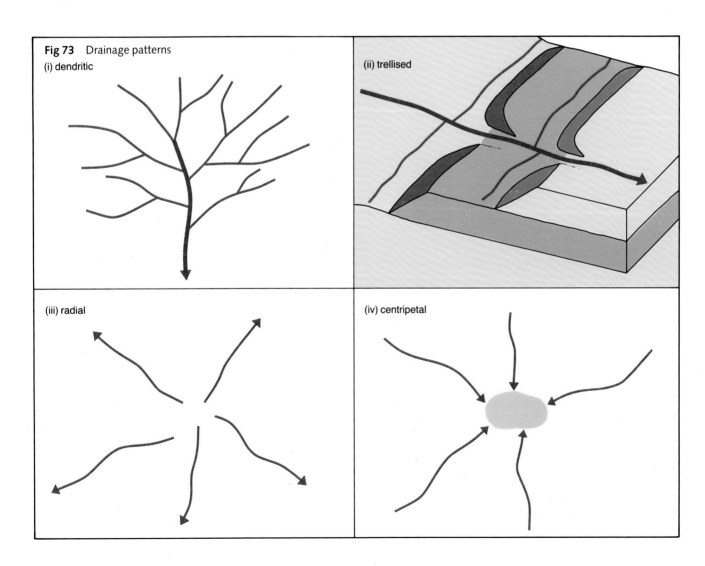

Fig 73   Drainage patterns
(i) dendritic
(ii) trellised
(iii) radial
(iv) centripetal

How does the river system work?

ENQUIRY

1 Which parts of the river system shown in Fig 74 are inputs and which are outputs?
2 Explain the different ways in which water gets into a river.
3 Water which does not get into a river straight away is said to be "stored". Where is water being stored in Fig 74?
4 What factors are likely to affect the regime of a river?

Fig 74 The river system

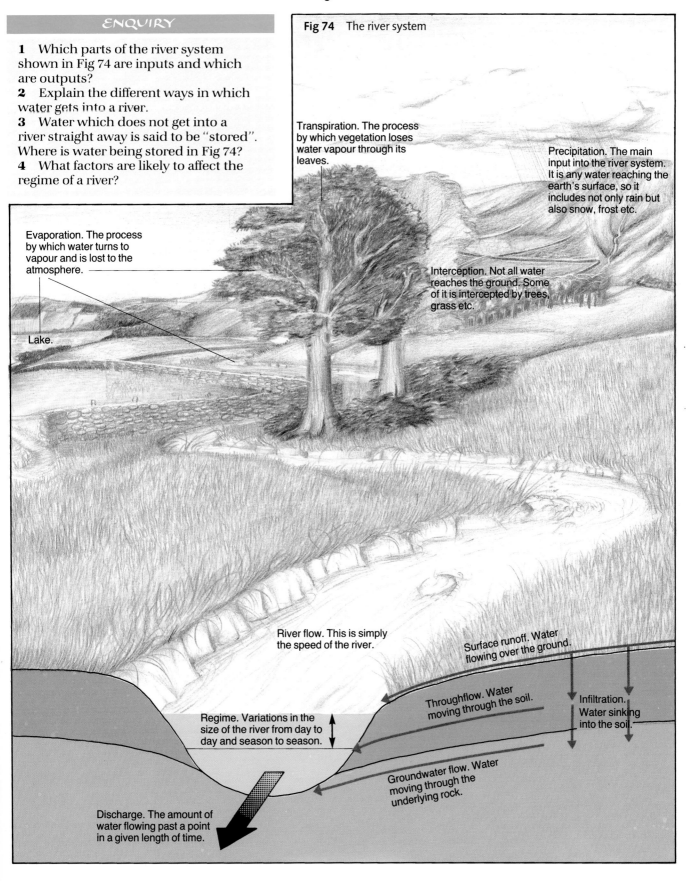

Transpiration. The process by which vegetation loses water vapour through its leaves.

Precipitation. The main input into the river system. It is any water reaching the earth's surface, so it includes not only rain but also snow, frost etc.

Evaporation. The process by which water turns to vapour and is lost to the atmosphere.

Interception. Not all water reaches the ground. Some of it is intercepted by trees, grass etc.

Lake.

River flow. This is simply the speed of the river.

Surface runoff. Water flowing over the ground.

Throughflow. Water moving through the soil.

Infiltration. Water sinking into the soil.

Regime. Variations in the size of the river from day to day and season to season.

Groundwater flow. Water moving through the underlying rock.

Discharge. The amount of water flowing past a point in a given length of time.

Investigating the River System

INFILTRATION SURVEY

Aim To find out how different factors affect infiltration rates.

Equipment Infiltration ring. Mallet. Water container. Watch. An infiltration ring is easy to make. The one in Fig 75 is simply a large tin can with the top and bottom removed. Jagged edges can be a problem, so be careful. Alternatively, a length of plastic pipe with a diameter of about 15 cm could be used. Draw a line around the inside of the ring 3 cm from the bottom. Then, draw and number a scale line 10 cm long. A piece of white tape can make this job easier.

Method Choose an area with a range of conditions, for example one with variations in soil cover (e.g. flower bed, grass, trees), soil type (e.g. clay soil, sandy soil, peat) and degree of slope (e.g. steep, gentle). Parks are often a good location but get permission from the park attendant first! Draw a sketch map of the area and mark onto it the sites where you are going to measure the infiltration rate (see Fig 76 for an example). At each site make a detailed note of the conditions. Knock the infiltration ring into the ground down to the 3 cm mark. Fill it with water to the top of the scale. Note the depth of water in the infiltration ring at the end of every minute. Carry on until the water has drained away or until it has stopped sinking in (the saturation point).

(A different way of carrying out this investigation would be to choose one site and measure its infiltration rate over a period of time, noting changes such as how long since it last rained.)

Presentation of Results Make a best copy of your map and descriptions. Draw a composite line graph of your results like the one in Fig 77.

Interpretation and Explanation Which sites had a high infiltration rate? Which sites had a low infiltration rate? Were the infiltration rates similar in any way? What were the main differences? Try to explain your observations.

Conclusion Summarise the ways in which the factors you looked at affected infiltration rates.

Limitations Did you have any problems when you were carrying out your investigation? If you were to repeat this study are there any ways in which you would try to improve it?

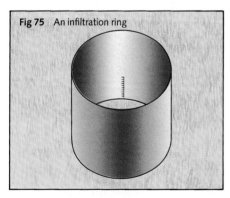

Fig 75 An infiltration ring

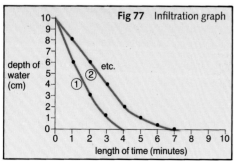

Fig 77 Infiltration graph

depth of water (cm)

etc.

length of time (minutes)

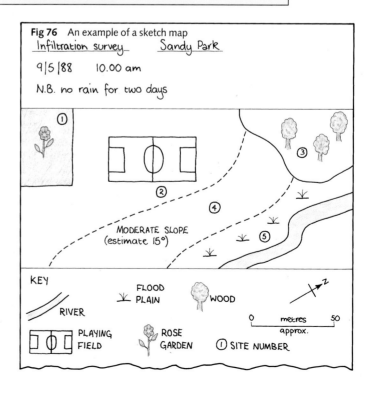

Fig 76 An example of a sketch map

Infiltration survey   Sandy Park

9/5/88   10.00 am

N.B. no rain for two days

MODERATE SLOPE (estimate 15°)

KEY

RIVER

FLOOD PLAIN

WOOD

PLAYING FIELD

ROSE GARDEN

SITE NUMBER

0   metres   50
approx.

River Surveys

A wide range of surveys can be carried out on a river. Four ideas are explained below. They could be investigated separately or they could be combined. Once you have collected and presented your results you will need to interpret and explain them. In your conclusion you should return to the aim(s) of your survey and summarise your main findings. Your final section should be about the limitations of your investigation.

Although the following studies are called river surveys, small streams are much easier and safer to investigate. Always be careful and never work alone.

TO STUDY THE SPEED OF A RIVER

Three ideas which could be tested are:

● does speed vary as you move downstream?
● does speed vary across the width of a stream?
● does speed vary with depth?

A simple way of finding out the speed of a river is as follows –

1 Measure out a 10 metre section of river.
2 Place a small dog biscuit in the main current of the river and time how long it takes to cover the 10 metres. (The advantages of a dog biscuit are that it is cheap and it has "neutral buoyancy" which means that it is carried along without sinking and at the same speed as the river!)
3 Do this three times and work out the average.
4 The speed of the river in metres per second is simply 10 metres divided by the average time in seconds.

Another way of finding out the speed of a river is to use a flow meter. The one in Fig 78 has a dial which gives you a reading in metres per second. Measurements across the width of a stream can be taken quickly and easily and it is possible to study variations in speed with depth. However, flow meters are very expensive and borrowing one may be difficult.

Fig 78 Flow meter

TO STUDY THE SHAPE OF A RIVER'S CHANNEL

To do this you will need a tape measure and a long ruler –

1 Stretch the tape measure across the river.
2 Measure and record the depth of the water at 30 cm intervals. (Always begin with the left hand bank looking downstream.)
3 Use your results to plot a cross section on graph paper like the one in Fig 80.

Fig 79
Surveying a river's cross section

TO STUDY A RIVER'S DISCHARGE

A river's discharge is measured in cubic metres per second (cumecs). A simple formula is used to calculate it:

discharge = speed (metres/second) × cross sectional area (square metres)

It is therefore necessary to measure the speed of the river and to survey its cross section. Its cross sectional area can be worked out from a graph like the one in Fig 80. In this example 100 small squares make up a square metre. So, all you have to do to get the cross sectional area is to count up the number of small squares and divide by 100.

It is interesting to see what happens to a river's discharge as you move downstream.

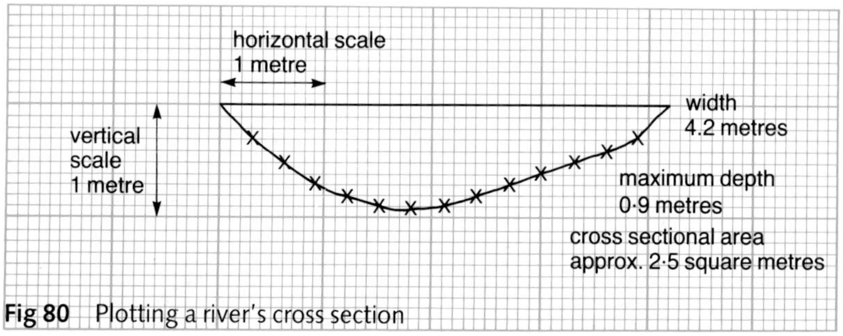

Fig 80 Plotting a river's cross section

horizontal scale 1 metre

vertical scale 1 metre

width 4.2 metres

maximum depth 0·9 metres

cross sectional area approx. 2·5 square metres

Fig 81 A river's load

FLOATATION LOAD material floating on the surface

SUSPENSION LOAD fine particles held in the water

TRACTION LOAD stones, gravel etc. rolled along the bed of the river

SOLUTION LOAD material dissolved in the water

Fig 82 Sampling the traction load of a river

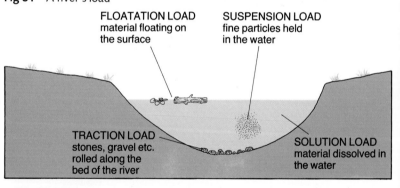

TO STUDY THE LOAD OF A RIVER

The load of a river is the material it is transporting (moving). The different types of load are shown in Fig 81. Any floatation load can simply be recorded. Any traction load can be measured at fixed intervals across the river (Fig 82). If a sample of water is taken it can be filtered to see if there is any suspension load. If you have access to a laboratory you could then evaporate the sample to see if there is any solution load.

Again, it is interesting to see how a river's load changes as you move downstream.

Hydrographs

A hydrograph is a line graph which shows river discharge over a given period of time.

Annual hydrographs show variations in a whole year's discharge. Fig 83 shows the River Nile's annual hydrograph. The tremendous increase in discharge in August and September is mainly the result of heavy rain in the Ethiopian Highlands swelling one of its tributaries, the Blue Nile, to 40 times its minimum discharge.

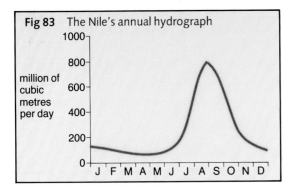

Fig 83 The Nile's annual hydrograph

Before river management schemes were introduced the Nile burst its banks every August, irrigating its flood plain and leaving a layer of fertile silt. Construction of the Aswan High Dam in Egypt began in 1960 and downstream of the dam the annual flood is now completely under control. There are major schemes upstream as well. However, the hydrograph in Fig 83 shows average conditions and these schemes are unable to cope with years of unusually heavy rainfall, such as in 1988 (Fig 84).

Flood hydrographs show a river's discharge after a period of heavy rain (Fig 85). The flood appears as a peak above the base (normal) flow. The height of the peak and the time the river takes to reach this peak both depend on a number of factors which vary considerably from one river to another. However, floods have such a major impact on our activities that a thorough knowledge of these factors is important in order that we may predict floods and decide how best to control them.

Factors affecting River Hydrographs

As a general rule, the greater the rainfall the greater is the discharge. However, the distribution and type of rainfall is important to the shape of the hydrograph; for example, occasional heavy storms produce distinct peaks in discharge whereas well-distributed rainfall produces a more gentle hydrograph.

Impermeable rocks and soils with low infiltration rates result in rapid surface runoff and

Fig 84 The Nile flood, 1988

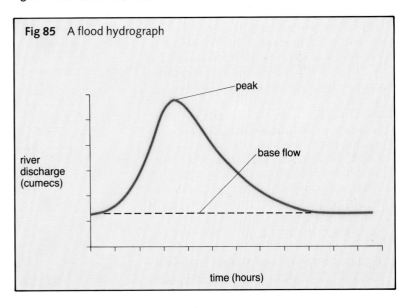

Fig 85 A flood hydrograph

therefore higher peaks in discharge in comparison with permeable rocks and soils with high infiltration rates.

Interception by vegetation slows down the time it takes for rain to get into the river system; consequently, a lack of vegetation results in peaked hydrographs.

Low drainage densities mean greater peaks because it takes less time for water to get into the main channel. For the same reason, the smaller the basin the greater the peaks. The shape of the basin is important because it affects the distance and therefore the time it takes for water to reach the main channel. The steeper the slope of the basin the greater are the peaks because surface runoff is more rapid.

The most obvious way in which we affect hydrographs is through river management schemes such as dam construction. However, surface runoff is greater in towns and cities compared with the surrounding countryside because of the impermeable nature of roads and pavements etc. As a result, peaks in the hydrograph become much greater and this can lead to flooding downstream of a settlement. There are also many ways in which farming can increase surface runoff e.g. by leaving fields bare in winter.

ENQUIRY

1 What is a hydrograph?
2 What is the difference between average discharge at the start of July compared with the start of August on the River Nile? What is the river's average annual peak discharge?
3 What were some of the human consequences of the 1988 Nile flood?
4 Explain the difference between an annual hydrograph and a flood hydrograph.
5 Complete a copy of Fig 86 by using words and/or phrases from the following list – heavy storms, well-distributed rainfall, permeable, impermeable, low, high, dense, little, high, low, large, small, long and thin, short and round, steep, gentle, flood control schemes, no river management, open countryside, urban settlement, pastoral, arable.
6 On a graph outline like the one in Fig 87 plot the rainfall statistics and the two river hydrographs. Describe the different ways in which the rivers responded to the storm. River A is in an area of impermeable rock used for sheep grazing while River B is in an area of permeable rock used for forestry. How does this information help to explain the different response of the rivers to the storm?
7 Why do you think predicting floods is difficult?

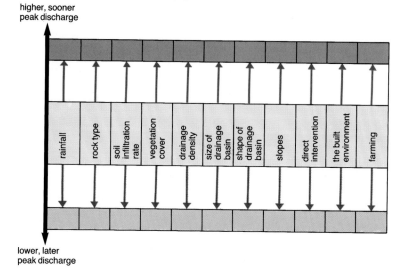

Fig 86 Factors affecting river hydrographs

higher, sooner peak discharge

rainfall · rock type · soil infiltration rate · vegetation cover · drainage density · size of drainage basin · shape of drainage basin · slopes · direct intervention · the built environment · farming

lower, later peak discharge

Fig 87 Two flood hydrographs

time (hours)	0-2	2-4	4-6	6-8	8-10	10-12	12-14	14-16	16-18	18-20	20-22	22-24	24-26
Rain mm	5	15	20	30	20	10	5	–	–	–	–	–	–

time (hours)	0	2	4	6	8	10	12	14	16	18	20	22	24
river A Discharge (cumecs)	20	30	50	80	150	200	120	70	50	30	20	20	20
river B (cumecs) Discharge	10	15	20	30	40	50	60	70	75	70	55	40	30

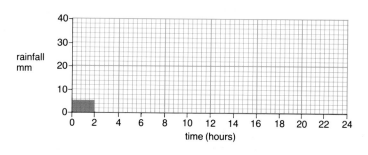

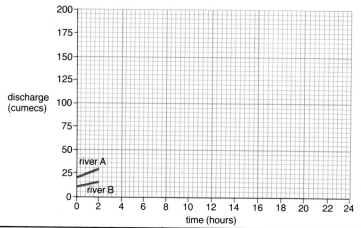

How do rivers shape the land?

River Processes

Rivers carry out three main processes – erosion, transportation and deposition. You can think of these as the "jobs" the river does.

1   Erosion

Erosion is the process by which rocks are worn away. A river erodes in the following ways:

- **Hydraulic action.**   This is the sheer power of running water wearing away the bed and banks of the river. Running water can also compress air into cracks or holes in the banks of a river and make them larger.
- **Abrasion (corrasion).**   This involves the river rolling or hurling rock fragments, gravel etc against its bed and banks which are chipped and scratched away as a result.
- **Solution (corrosion).**   This is when the river dissolves the rocks it is flowing across.

Another important aspect of erosion is **attrition**. This is the process by which rock fragments are broken up as they knock into each other. It reduces the size of the river's load and provides material for abrasion.

2   Transportation

This is the process by which the river moves its load (see page 38). It can only do this if it has enough energy.

Fig 88   The power of running water

Fig 89   Deposition

3   Deposition

If a river lacks the energy needed to carry its load it will deposit it (dump it) in order to keep flowing.

The main aim of a river is to cut an efficient course from its source to its mouth. The ideal "long profile" is a smooth curve like the one in Fig 90. The balance between erosion and deposition varies along this profile. Erosion is more common in the upper section where the river's gradient (slope) is greater and where it has more energy. Deposition is more common in the lower section where the river's gradient is gentle and where it has less energy. In the middle section erosion and deposition are more finely balanced.

However, rates of erosion and deposition vary considerably from day to day and season to season. In dry weather rivers in their upper section may have to deposit their load in order to keep flowing. On the other hand, when the river is full erosion can be the most important process even in the lower section.

ENQUIRY

1   Draw and label a diagram to show the main river processes of erosion, transportation and deposition.
2   Use a whole page to make a copy of Fig 90; (you will be adding details to this diagram as part of later Enquiries). Label onto it the most important processes found in each stage.

Fig 90   The long profile of a river

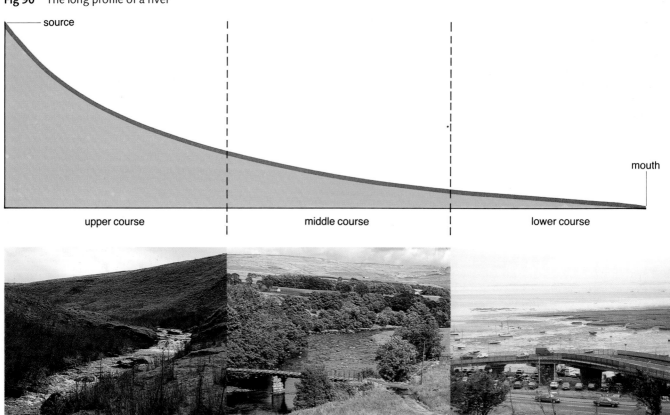

source

upper course   middle course   lower course

mouth

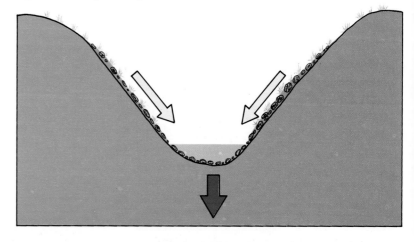

River features – the upper section

'V'-shaped Valleys

'V'-shaped valleys like the one in Fig 91 are a characteristic feature of the upper section of a river. They are the result of rapid downward erosion combined with mass movement on the valley sides (see Section 2.2). Mass movement also provides material for abrasion.

Gorges

If there is little or no mass movement, or if the rate of downward erosion is very much faster than the rate of mass movement, the sides of a valley remain vertical. The result is a gorge.

Fig 91   'V'-shaped valley

Interlocking Spurs

As the river flows away from its source it begins to swing from side to side. Of course, it is still rapidly cutting downwards. The result is a series of hills (spurs) which fit together (interlock) like the pieces of a jigsaw puzzle (Fig 92).

Fig 92 Interlocking spurs

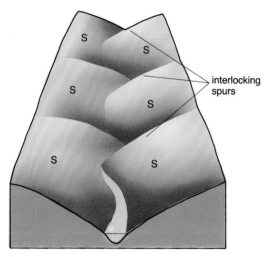

S = spur

Rapids

Rapids are areas of fast-flowing, turbulent water. They form when the bed of a river is made up of hard and soft rocks (Fig 93). The soft rocks are worn away more quickly leaving the hard rocks sticking up into the river channel.

Waterfalls

These sudden falls of water can be formed in a number of different ways – for example, they could be the result of water plunging over the side of a rift valley (see page 14), or the side of a glaciated valley (see page 58). However, many waterfalls are the result of a bed of hard rock overlying a bed of soft rock. They begin as rapids but as more and more of the soft rock is eroded the drop becomes steeper until it is vertical. At the base of the waterfall hydraulic action erodes a deep plunge pool (Fig 94).

The river continues to erode the soft layer of rock as it goes over the fall. As a result, the hard layer of rock is undercut. Eventually, the overhang collapses and the process repeats itself. In this way the waterfall retreats upstream leaving a gorge downstream (Fig 95).

Fig 93 Rapids

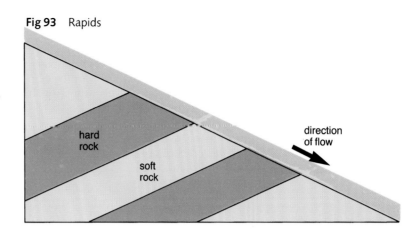

hard rock

soft rock

direction of flow

Fig 94 Cross section of a waterfall

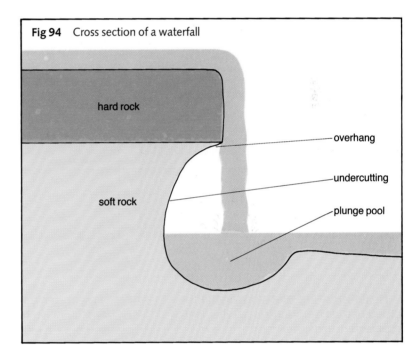

hard rock

soft rock

overhang

undercutting

plunge pool

Fig 95 Waterfall retreat

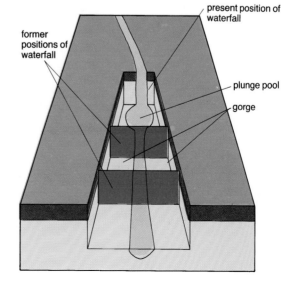

present position of waterfall

former positions of waterfall

plunge pool

gorge

Pot-holes

Geographers use the term pot-holes to describe small depressions found in the bed of a river (Fig 96). However, the term is also used by underground cavers to describe swallow holes or sinks (see page 91). Pot-holes form when rock fragments get caught up in eddies (circular currents). As they are swirled round the process of abrasion "drills" into the rock. They are often found downstream of a waterfall because here the water is fast flowing and turbulent.

Fig 96 Pot-hole (evorsion hollow)

Meanders, Bluffs and Slip-off Slopes

Meanders – the loops and curves in the course of a river – are found in all three sections of a river's long profile. In the upper section they are relatively small but they already show a range of features.

As the river flows round the meander the current is swung to the outside of the bend by centrifugal force. This means that the erosive power of the river is concentrated on the outside bend. The river's channel is eroded more deeply and the banks are undercut, leaving an overhang. When this overhang eventually collapses a small river cliff, known as a bluff, is formed. On the inside of the bend the current is much weaker and deposition takes place. The small beach which results is known as a slip-off slope (Fig 97).

Fig 97 Meanders, bluffs and slip-off slopes

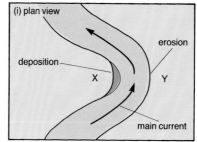
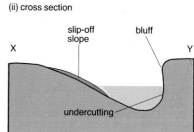

ENQUIRY

1 Re-draw Fig 93 to show what the bed of the river would look like after a period of erosion.
2 Explain, with the aid of diagrams, how waterfalls are formed and why they retreat upstream.
3 Make a sketch of Fig 98. Label onto it

a meander, a bluff and a slip-off slope.
4 Label each of the features found in the upper section of a river onto your copy of Fig 90, page 42. Add a brief definition to each feature and state whether it is caused by erosion or deposition.

Fig 98
Cowside Beck near Arncliffe, North Yorkshire

River features – the middle section

Some of the features found in the upper section of a river are also found in its middle section. Rapids and waterfalls are still present but they are less common. Meanders are a larger and more important feature, and bluffs and slip-off slopes are still found. However, there are some important differences as well.

Open 'V'-shaped Valleys and Narrow Flood Plains

The most striking difference is that the narrow 'V'-shaped valley and the interlocking spurs of the upper section are no longer there. Instead, the sides of the valley are parallel and the bottom of the valley is flat. The river itself has brought about these changes by eroding the spurs (Fig 99).

The flood plain forms when the river spills out onto the flat valley bottom and deposits a layer of silt and alluvium.

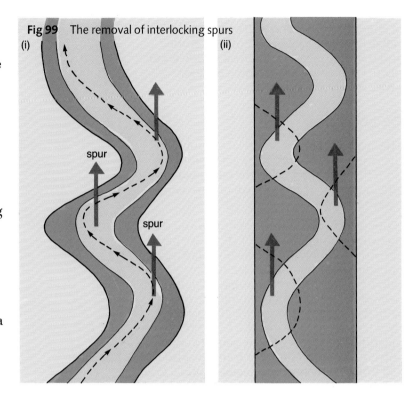

Fig 99 The removal of interlocking spurs

(i)

spur

spur

(ii)

ENQUIRY

1 Copy the diagrams in Fig 99 and add labels to them to explain how the river removes its interlocking spurs.
2 Complete Fig 90, page 42 for the middle section of a river in the same way as you did for the upper section in the previous Enquiry.

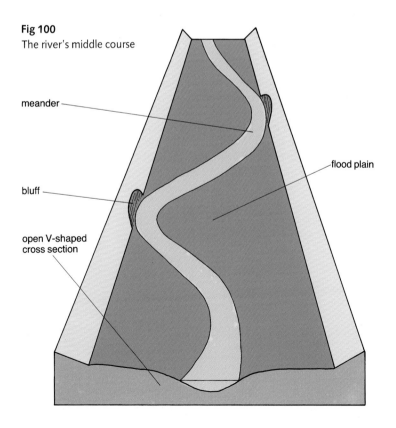

Fig 100
The river's middle course

meander

bluff

open V-shaped
cross section

flood plain

River features – the lower section

This section of a river's course has a number of characteristic features. The sides of the valley have often been completely eroded and the river meanders across a wide flood plain. Deposition has become a major process.

Ox-bow Lakes

These are crescent shaped lakes found on the river's flood plain. They get their name from the U-shaped yoke (the collar which attaches animals to a plough or cart) worn by oxen.

Ox-bow lakes are another feature formed by the work of meanders (Fig 101). As we have already seen, erosion is concentrated on the outside bend of the meander at place X. Undercutting and collapse results in the neck of the meander becoming narrower until it is breached at place Y. The river can then flow straight across the neck of the meander instead of flowing round it. With no current, the water at the entrance to and the exit from the meander at places R and S loses energy and deposits its load. This blocks off the meander completely, forming the ox-bow lake. Eventually, the ox-bow lake itself may silt up and become vegetated; if this happens it is known as a meander scroll.

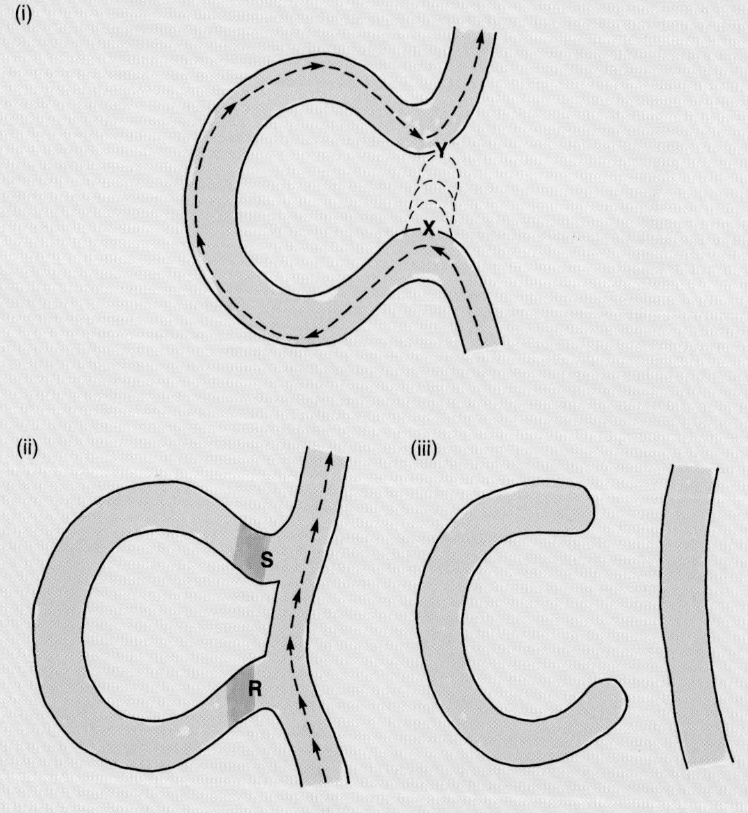

Braiding

Braiding is the process by which a river channel splits into two or more parts which then join up again. It does this when it is no longer able to carry its load. By depositing material it is able to regain energy and keep flowing. Examples of braids as well as ox-bow lakes can be seen in Fig 102.

Fig 101 The formation of ox-bow lakes

(i)

(ii)   (iii)

Fig 102   River Add, Argyleshire

Levées

Rivers in their lower section are often lined by raised banks. These may have been built deliberately to prevent flooding or they may have formed naturally, as levées, at least in the first instance.

When the river spills onto its flood plain the water loses energy quickly and deposits its load. Larger, heavier material is deposited first, nearest to the river. Smaller, lighter material is deposited further away. When the river floods again the process is repeated and in this way a levée builds up (Fig 103).

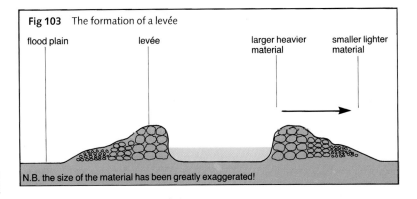

Fig 103   The formation of a levée

flood plain   levée   larger heavier   smaller lighter
                                              material   material

N.B. the size of the material has been greatly exaggerated!

Deltas

A delta is a low-lying area of land at the mouth of a river where it enters the sea or a lake. A delta forms if the currents in the sea or lake are too weak to carry away the material being deposited by the river. As the delta builds up the river is forced to split into a number of smaller streams, known a distributaries.

There are two main types of delta – **arcuate** and **bird's foot**. Arcuate deltas, such as the Nile delta (Fig 104), are fan-shaped. They are made up of sand and gravel as well as finer sediments such as silt and alluvium.

If the sediments are very fine and the currents are very weak the river's distributaries are able to build out into the sea or lake without being disturbed at all. The result is a bird's foot delta, such as the Mississippi delta (Fig 105). Levées usually build up on either side of the distributary.

Fig 104   Satellite image of the Nile delta

Fig 105   The Mississippi delta (satellite image)

Alluvial Fans

If there is a sudden reduction in the gradient (slope) of a river it loses energy and deposits some of its load. This can lead to the formation of an alluvial fan. As its name suggests it is fan-shaped, and it gets thinner in a downstream direction.

The alluvial fans in Fig 106 are at the base of the Panamint Mountains in Death Valley, California. They are a common feature in arid regions such as this because the rivers flow only for short periods of time (see Section 6) and so they lack the energy needed to transport their load across the flat plain at the foot of the mountains.

Fig 106
Alluvial fans

Changes in Base-level

Base-level means the lowest level a river can wear down to. This is usually the sea or an inland lake. If the base-level changes the river has to adjust to this new condition. The Ice Age (see Section 4) produced many such changes. During glacial periods water was stored in ice sheets and glaciers and the sea-level fell. During interglacials the ice melted, flowed back into the sea and caused the sea-level to rise. Other events, such as earth-quakes, can also cause a change in base-level.

Terraces

A fall in base-level means that a river has to wear downwards in order to get back to the smooth curve of its "ideal" long profile. As it does so it cuts into its own flood plain. The remnants of the flood plain are left as flat strips of land on the side of the valley – these are known as terraces (Fig 107). The break of slope where the terraces meet is known as a knick-point and it is often the location of rapids or of a waterfall. As the knick-point wears backwards the terraces extend up-stream, and as a result they can be found in any section of the river's long profile.

Estuaries

A rise in base-level floods the lower section of a river valley. The result is a wide, shallow river mouth known as an estuary. Estuaries are tidal and the deposition of silt can lead to the build-up of mud flats (Fig 108).

Fig 107   The formation of river terraces

(i) cross section

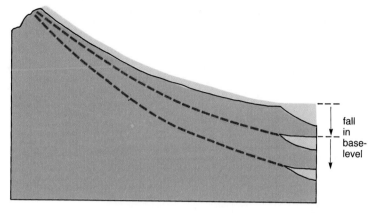

fall in base-level

(ii) a section of river valley

knick-point

Ⓣ = terrace

Fig 108   The Thames Estuary

Rivers and people

There are many ways in which we make use of rivers and their valleys. In turn, river systems require careful management or problems such as pollution can occur. Rivers can themselves pose problems for, or threaten, human activities – for example, they can be a barrier to communications, or lives and land can be lost in a flood.

No study of rivers is complete without considering their impact on the human environment. Some examples of how we make use of rivers and their valleys are shown in Fig 109. It would be a good idea to develop two or three of these themes into major case studies. Information about many of these is to be found in Discover Human Geography.

(i) (ii) (iii) (iv) (v) (vi) (vii) (viii)

Fig 109 Rivers and people

Rivers on O.S. maps

1 Mark onto a sketch map or tracing of Fig 110 the streams and rivers, the roads and settlements, and the areas of woodland.

2 Mark on the line of any watersheds that you can identify.

3 Work out the stream order of Hudeshope Beck at 947 290.

4 How would you describe the drainage pattern of Hudeshope Beck?

5 Compare the shape of the valley of Hudeshope Beck in 94 29 with the shape of the valley of the River Tees in 92 26. What do you think explains this difference?

6 Label onto your sketch map examples of any of the river features mentioned in Section 3.3 that you can identify.

7 What might explain the distributon of woodland in the valley of Hudeshope Beck (page 113 will help you with the answer)?

8 Describe the relationship between the river valleys and the roads and settlements.

9 What evidence of river management is there in 93 25?

10 What map evidence is there of past and present land-use?

Scale 1:50 000   Ordnance Survey **OS**

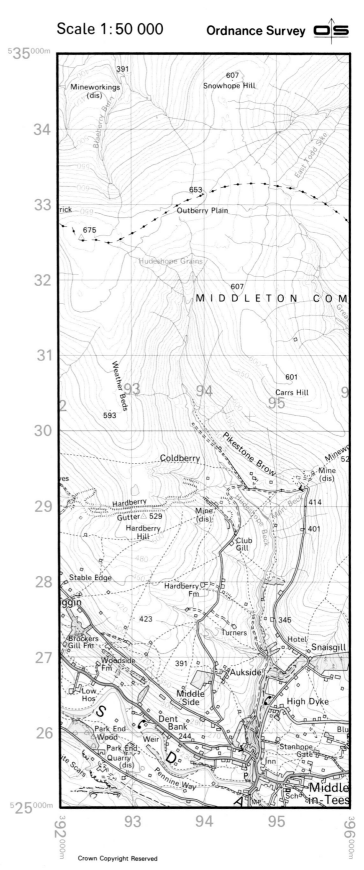

Fig 110

ICE

What was the Ice Age?

Today, about 10% of the earth's land surface is covered by ice. There are three types of permanent ice:

- **Ice sheets.** These are the large areas of thick ice found in Antarctica and Greenland (Fig 111).
- **Ice caps.** These are smaller areas of thick ice e.g Vatnajokull in Iceland.
- **Valley glaciers.** These are slow-moving rivers of ice (Fig 112).

However, at times during the Ice Age up to 30% of the earth's land surface was covered by ice. It began about 2 million years ago and there have been at least four (and possibly as many as twenty) very cold periods when the ice has advanced, separated by warmer periods when the ice has melted. Ice advances are called 'glaciations'; the last one began 70 000 years ago and ended 10 000 years ago. The warm periods are known as 'interglacials'; during these temperatures were like they are today, or even warmer.

The cause of these dramatic changes in the earth's climate is not known. There are a number of theories – for example, some scientists believe that variations in the sun's energy are responsible, while others think that the earth's orbit has changed so that for certain periods of time we are further away from the sun than we used to be. Until we know its cause it will not be possible to say whether or not the Ice Age has ended.

Fig 111   Antarctica

During glacial periods the sea-level fell by up to 135 metres because so much of the earth's water was stored on the land in the form of ice. One result of this fall in sea-level was that some countries which are now separated were joined by 'land bridges'. These land bridges made it easier for people to move from one region to another. The American Indians almost certainly walked across from Siberia when the Bering Straits was a land bridge. It is likely that the Aborigines reached Australia during the Ice Age when they could have migrated overland as far as Java or Kalimantan (Borneo) and then sailed across a much smaller stretch of water than there is today.

Fig 112   A valley glacier

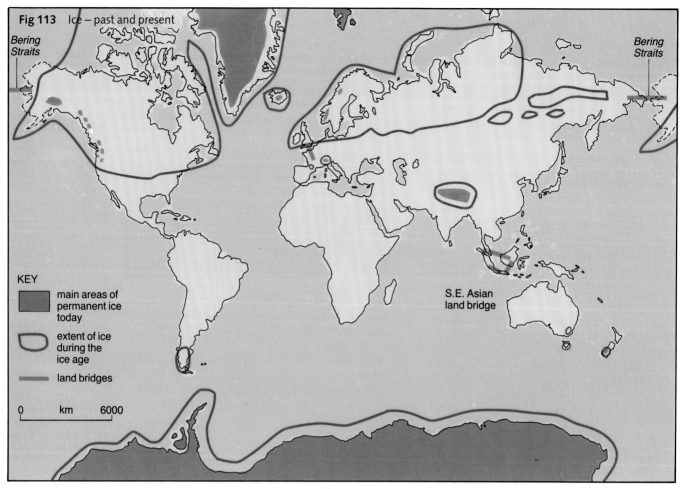

Fig 113   Ice – past and present

Bering Straits

Bering Straits

KEY

main areas of permanent ice today

extent of ice during the ice age

land bridges

0   km   6000

S.E. Asian land bridge

ENQUIRY

1 Name two countries in the northern hemisphere and one country and one continent in the southern hemisphere which have areas of permanent ice today.

2 What are the differences between an ice sheet, an ice cap and a valley glacier?

3 Define the following terms – Ice Age, glacial, interglacial, land bridge.

4 Why could our present climate be part of an interglacial?

5 How could the Ice Age have helped people to get to the British Isles?

6 Mark onto an outline map of the British Isles the limit of the last glaciation; the limit of the maximum glaciation; and the centres of ice dispersal. Shade in and label the parts of the country which were never glaciated. With the help of an atlas, name the centres of ice dispersal. Mark on the place where you live!

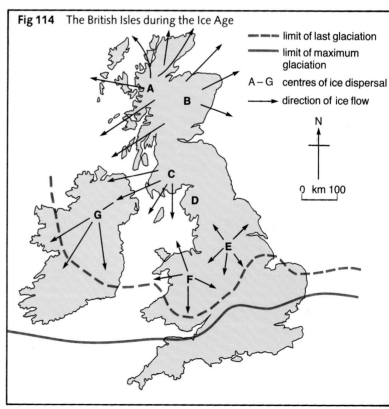

Fig 114   The British Isles during the Ice Age

— — — limit of last glaciation

——— limit of maximum glaciation

A – G   centres of ice dispersal

——▶ direction of ice flow

N

0   km   100

A

B

C

D

G

E

F

The Glacier System

A fresh layer of snow has a great deal of air trapped between its ice crystals. However, in glacial conditions snowfalls pile up on top of each other and squeeze this air out. Last year's snow is called nevee or firn and as it becomes more compressed it turns to ice. This build-up of ice is known as accumulation and very compressed ice appears blue (Fig 115).

When the surface of a glacier melts the process is known as ablation. Whereas accumulation is most likely to take place high in the mountains near the source of a glacier where temperatures are colder, ablation is more likely to take place at lower altitudes near the snout of a glacier where temperatures are warmer.

The balance between accumulation and ablation is clearly very important. If accumulation is greater than ablation the glacier will advance but if accumulation is less than ablation the glacier will retreat (Fig 116).

The speed at which a glacier moves varies between as little as 100 metres and as much as 7 kilometres a year. As it moves deep cracks, known as crevasses, open up in the ice because it is brittle. Experiments with markers have shown that the ice in the middle of a glacier moves faster than the ice at the sides or base (Fig 117).

Fig 115
Blue ice at the base of a glacier

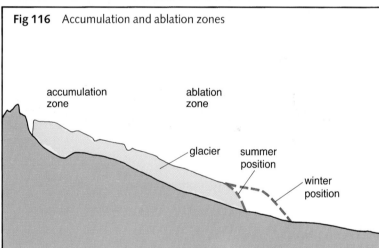

Fig 116 Accumulation and ablation zones

accumulation zone

ablation zone

glacier   summer position

winter position

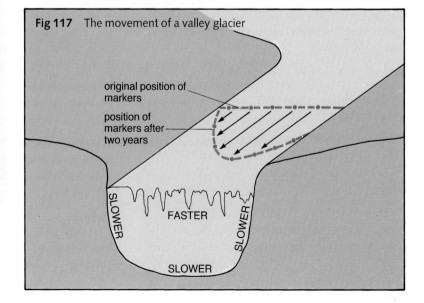

Fig 117 The movement of a valley glacier

original position of markers

position of markers after two years

SLOWER

FASTER

SLOWER

SLOWER

ENQUIRY

1 Draw a column 10 cm tall and 1 cm wide. Mark off the top two centimetres and label them 'This year's snow'. Mark off the next ½ centimetre and label it 'Nevee or firn – one year old'. Mark off the next 3½ centimetres and label the bottom of this section '25 years old'. Label the very bottom of the column '200 years old'. Give your diagram the title 'The accumulation of ice'.
2 Explain why the balance between accumulation and ablation is important. How will this balance vary between the seasons?
3 Why do you think glaciers move faster in the middle than at their sides or base?

How do glaciers shape the land?

Glacial Processes

Glaciers carry out the same three main processes as rivers – erosion, transportation and deposition. However, the individual processes involved are not always the same because of the different properties of ice and water.

1 Erosion

● **Abrasion.** This is when glaciers pick up rock fragments and drag them against the bed and sides of the valley which are scratched away as a result.
● **Bulldozing.** This is when the sheer power of the glacier breaks off rocks from the bed and sides of the valley, or when it moves already shattered material.
● **Plucking.** If the ice freezes onto a rock, the glacier will pull it away when it moves. This is known as plucking and it is more common in well-jointed rocks.

2 Transportation

Rock fragments which have fallen onto the side of a glacier are known as lateral moraine. A line of fragments in the middle of a glacier is known as a medial moraine. The fragments which collect at the snout of a glacier pile up to form a terminal moraine. Rock fragments can also be carried along within the ice (e.g. material which has fallen into a crevasse) or at the base of a glacier.

3 Deposition

When the ice melts it dumps its load. The result is a number of important features which are described and explained in the following pages.

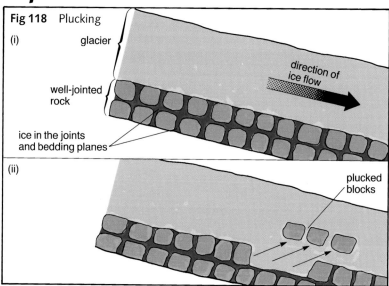

Fig 118   Plucking

(i) glacier

well-jointed rock

ice in the joints and bedding planes

direction of ice flow

(ii) plucked blocks

Fig 119   The different types of moraine

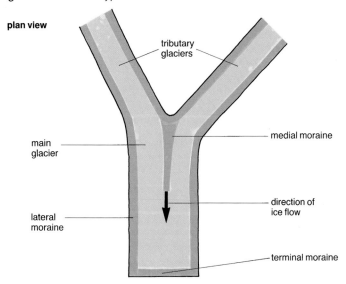

plan view

tributary glaciers

main glacier

lateral moraine

medial moraine

direction of ice flow

terminal moraine

Fig 120   Moraine on a valley glacier

ENQUIRY

1 In what ways are the processes of glacial erosion similar to the processes of river erosion?
2 Why do you think plucking is more common in well-jointed rocks?
3 What type of weathering do you think is responsible for much of the material which falls onto the surface of a glacier?
4 Explain how and why a medial moraine forms.
5 Make a sketch of the glacier in Fig 120. Label the different types of moraine, and any other glacial features you can identify.

Features of glacial erosion

Corries

Corries, which are also known as cwms or cirques, are bowl-shaped hollows with a steep back wall and a shallow lip. They are found high in the mountains and are the place where a glacier begins. Small 'corrie lakes' are often found in them.

Corries form when snow collects in a hollow and turns to ice. At first, the hollow is enlarged by freeze-thaw and by erosion as the ice slips. As the hollow becomes deeper, freeze-thaw and plucking become the main processes operating on the back wall while abrasion becomes the main process in the bowl of the corrie. The movement of the ice is rotational, and the lip forms because there is less erosion at the edge of the hollow than there is at the bottom of the hollow (Fig 121).

If two corries form back to back the land between them is worn away until only a knife-edge ridge is left, known as an arête. If three or more corries form back to back the result is a pyramidal peak (Fig 122).

Fig 121   The formation of a corrie

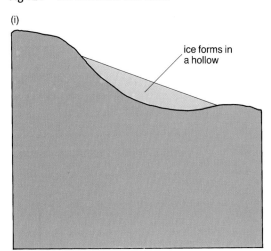

(i)

ice forms in a hollow

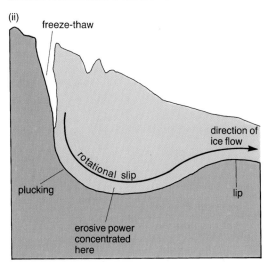

(ii)

freeze-thaw

direction of ice flow

rotational slip

plucking

lip

erosive power concentrated here

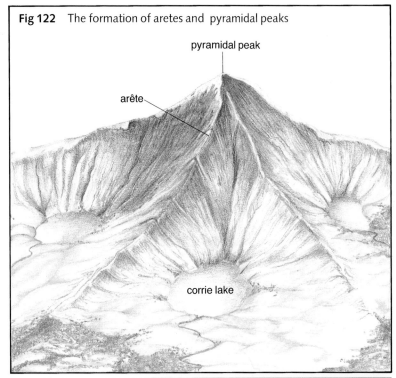

Fig 122   The formation of aretes and pyramidal peaks

pyramidal peak

arête

corrie lake

Fig 123   Corrie landscape

ENQUIRY

1   Explain, with the aid of diagrams, how a corrie forms.
2   Draw and label a sketch of the corrie in Fig 123.

'U'-shaped Valleys

River valleys in their upper sections are 'V'-shaped or gorge-like (see page 42). However, glaciers change this shape into a 'U' because they erode the sides as well as the bottom of the valley (Fig 124).

Truncated Spurs and Hanging Valleys

Ice is much less flexible than water. As a result, a valley glacier is unable to flow around interlocking spurs in the way that a river can. Instead, the erosive power of the glacier is concentrated on the spurs and eventually they are worn away leaving the valley with straight, smooth sides (Fig 125). The eroded spurs are known as truncated spurs.

Fig 124   The formation of a 'U'-shaped valley

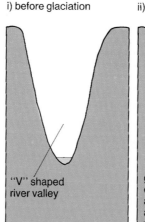
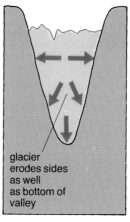
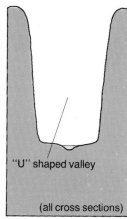

i) before glaciation   ii) during glaciation   iii) after glaciation

"V" shaped river valley

glacier erodes sides as well as bottom of valley

"U" shaped valley

(all cross sections)

Fig 125   'U'-shaped valley

Before glaciation a tributary valley would have joined a main valley at the same height (Fig 126 i). During glaciation the main valley would have been occupied by a large, powerful glacier which would have removed the interlocking spurs and eroded a deep valley (Fig 126 ii). The tributary valley would have been occupied by a small, less powerful glacier which would only have been able to erode a small valley. As a result, after glaciation the tributary valley finds itself 'hanging' high above the main valley. If there is a stream in the hanging valley it plunges over the edge as a waterfall, depositing an alluvial fan on the main valley floor (Fig 126 iii).

ENQUIRY

1   Explain why glaciated valleys are 'U'-shaped and not 'V'-shaped.
2   Copy the diagrams in Fig 126. Add your own labels to them to explain how truncated spurs and hanging valleys form.

Fig 126   Truncated spurs and hanging valleys

(i)

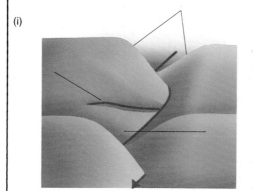

(ii)

(iii)

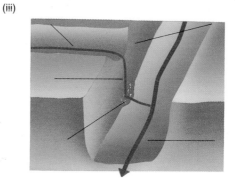

Fig 127   Hanging valley

Roches Moutonnées and Striations

When a glacier meets a hard outcrop of rock in the valley floor it may not be able to remove it completely. However, the glacier does change the outcrop's shape to form a feature known as a roche moutonnée (Figs 128 and 130).

The upstream side of the outcrop is smoothed and scratched as the glacier flows over it. The scratches, known as striations, are deeper at one end than the other because the rock fragments are ground down as they are dragged along. They are not only found on roches moutonnées but are a common feature of all glaciated rock surfaces (Fig 129).

The downstream side of the outcrop is plucked by the glacier as it moves over it. As a result, it remains steep and jagged.

Crag and Tail

If a hard outcrop of rock in the valley floor is in front of soft rock, a feature known as a crag and tail may form (Fig 131). The glacier is unable to erode the hard rock completely. Some of the ice flows over the top of the outcrop while the rest flows round the sides. The soft rock immediately behind the outcrop is therefore protected and it is not until the glacier joins up further downstream that it can start eroding its deep valley again.

Castle Rock in Edinburgh is a famous example of a crag and tail (Fig 132). The crag (the site of the castle) is a plug of hard volcanic rock. This has protected the tail of softer limestone and sandstone (the site of the Royal Mile).

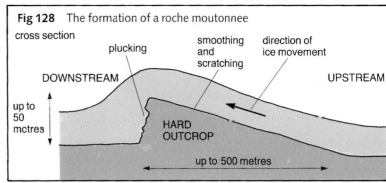

Fig 128   The formation of a roche moutonnee
cross section

DOWNSTREAM   UPSTREAM
plucking   smoothing and scratching   direction of ice movement
up to 50 metres
HARD OUTCROP
up to 500 metres

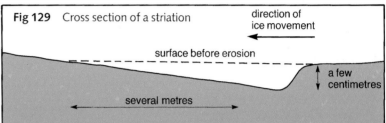

Fig 129   Cross section of a striation
direction of ice movement
surface before erosion
a few centimetres
several metres

Fig 130   Roche moutonnee

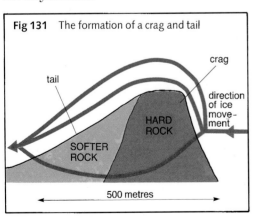

Fig 131   The formation of a crag and tail
tail
crag
direction of ice movement
HARD ROCK
SOFTER ROCK
500 metres

Fig 132
Castle Rock, Edinburgh

ENQUIRY

1 Which process of glacial erosion is responsible for striations?
2 Why are striations useful for working out the direction of ice flow?

3 In what ways is the formation of a roche moutonnée and a crag and tail a) similar and b) different?

Ribbon Lakes

The long, thin lakes found in many glaciated valleys are known as ribbon lakes (Fig 133). Streams flowing into these lakes deposit sediment which slowly builds up to form areas of flat land. This can be very important for farming in a region of otherwise steep slopes.

Fjords

Fjords are glaciated valleys which have been worn down to the sea and which have been drowned by the rise in sea-level since the ice melted. They have steep sides and are very deep, although there is a shallow threshold at their mouth (Fig 134).

There are excellent examples of fjords on the west coast of Norway and the south west coast of South Island, New Zealand (Figs 135 and 136). Both these places have high mountains very close to the sea. This helps to explain the steep slopes and the depth of the fjords because the glaciers would have been coming down from a great height and would therefore have been very powerful. Freeze-thaw is also thought to have been important because it would have shattered the rocks on the floor of the valley, leaving the glacier simply to bulldoze them away.

The shallow threshold is still something of a mystery. However, it probably marks the place at which the glacier ran out of energy, perhaps because it met the sea and began to melt. In some cases it could be a terminal moraine.

Fig 133   Ribbon lake

Fig 134   Cross section of a fjord

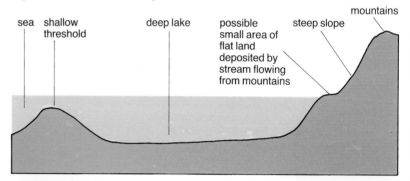

sea   shallow threshold   deep lake   possible small area of flat land deposited by stream flowing from mountains   steep slope   mountains

Fig 135   The Hardanger Fjord, Norway

ENQUIRY

1   What is a ribbon lake? Why are most ribbon lakes becoming smaller?

2   Draw a large diagram of a fjord. Add labels to your diagram to explain what a fjord is and how they form.

3   In what ways do you think people can make use of a fjord environment?

4   Choose either the west coast of Norway or the south west coast of South Island, New Zealand. Draw a sketch map of the fjord coastline of your chosen region and label the example shown in either Fig 135 or Fig 136.

Fig 136   Milford Sound, New Zealand

Features of glacial deposition

Erratics

An erratic is a rock or boulder which has been moved by a glacier and deposited (dumped) somewhere else. The Norber Rocks (see page 24) are a famous example. Here, the sandstone boulders have been moved from Crummack Dale only a few kilometres away. Some erratics have been moved much longer distances e.g. rocks from Oslo in Norway can be found along the Yorkshire coast.

Moraine

Moraine is a deposit of angular rock fragments. The different types of moraine are explained on page 56. When the ice melts the material is dumped and it forms low hills along the floor, sides, middle or at the front of the glacier (Fig 137). These deposits are very loose and unconsolidated and most of them have been affected by weathering, mass movement and river action since the ice melted.

Boulder Clay (also known as Till)

This is a mixture of angular rock fragments in a mass of clay (Fig 138). The clay is the result of rock fragments being ground down underneath the ice. Large areas of the country have a covering of boulder clay. It is difficult to farm because it is heavy and sticky but in many parts of the country boulder clay soils have been successfully improved and have become areas of rich farmland e.g. the boulder clay soils of East Anglia.

In a number of places it forms a series of low hills known as drumlins (Figs 139 and 140). The exact cause of drumlins is not fully understood but it is almost certain that they were deposited while the ice was still moving; this would help to account for their streamlined shape.

Fig 137
A terminal moraine

Fig 138
Boulder clay

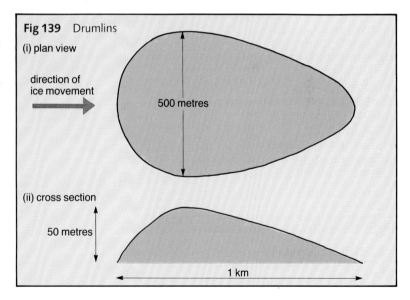

Fig 139   Drumlins

(i) plan view

direction of ice movement

500 metres

(ii) cross section

50 metres

1 km

Fig 140
Drumlins near Ribblesdale, North Yorkshire

Fluvioglacial Deposition

This means deposition by water, streams and rivers associated with melting ice. Fluvioglacial deposits are mainly sand and gravel. The particles are rounded by the process of attrition and because water is involved the deposits are often in layers.

Kames and Kame Terraces

A kame is a mixture of sand and gravel which has been deposited by meltwater in a crevasse. A kame terrace is a ridge of this material along the side of a valley which has been deposited by a meltwater lake at the edge of an ice sheet or glacier.

Eskers

When the ice begins to melt streams often form on the surface of the ice or even within the ice itself. There is usually more material than the streams can carry so they deposit their load as a long, meandering ridge of sand and gravel known as an esker.

Outwash Plains

The meltwater streams flowing away from the front of an ice sheet or the snout of a glacier are also 'super charged' with sand and gravel and they deposit their load as a low flat plain. These can stretch for many kilometres and they are crossed by river channels which are constantly braiding in order to regain energy. These deposits are naturally infertile and it is only in places where they have been heavily improved with fertilizers that they can be used for farming e.g. the Goodsands area of Norfolk.

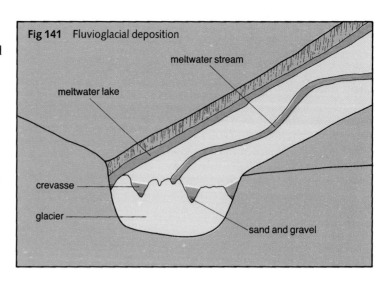

Fig 141 Fluvioglacial deposition

meltwater stream

meltwater lake

crevasse

glacier

sand and gravel

Fig 142   Glacial and fluvioglacial deposition – a summary table

Feature	Glacial or fluvioglacial?	Angular or rounded fragments?	Mixed or layered material?	Potential for farming – good or bad?
Erratic				
Moraine				
Boulder clay				
Kame or kame terrace				
Esker				
Outwash plain				

ENQUIRY

1 With the aid of diagrams, describe and explain how drumlins form.
2 Copy and complete Fig 142. What does this tell us about the main differences between glacial and fluvioglacial deposits?
3 Draw a sketch of what you think the landscape in Fig 141 will look like after the ice has completely melted.
4 Make a sketch of Fig 143. Label as many features of glacial and fluvioglacial erosion and deposition as you can identify.

Fig 143
Fox glacier,
New Zealand

Periglacial features

'Peri' is a prefix which means 'round'. Periglacial features are therefore found round the edge of an ice sheet or glacier. These areas are very cold and barren. The tundra regions of North America and the north of Europe and Asia still experience such conditions (Fig 144). It is an important environment to study because much of southern Britain was like this during the ice age and periglacial features have helped to form the landscape of this part of the country.

A major feature of the periglacial environment is permafrost which means permanently frozen ground. This can reach a depth of 300 metres. However, the top one or two metres may thaw during the short tundra summer and this is known as the active layer.

Fig 144   Tundra landscape

Ice Wedges

In the winter when temperatures often fall to as low as − 30 degrees Celsius the ground contracts and splits open. Snow and debris falls into these cracks. In the summer when the weather is warmer the cracks close up. However, they are unable to close fully because of the material which has collected in them. During the following winter the cracks open again, more snow and debris falls into them and the process is repeated (Fig 145). These features can be seen in many British gravel pits where the triangular shaped wedges of finer material stand out clearly against the coarser sand and gravel background (Fig 146).

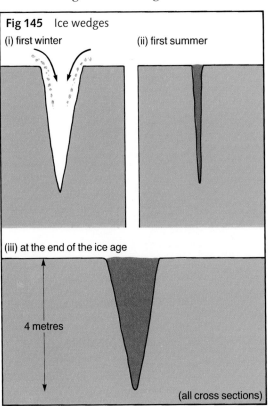

Fig 145   Ice wedges

(i) first winter

(ii) first summer

(iii) at the end of the ice age

4 metres

(all cross sections)

Fig 146   An ice wedge

Pingos

A pingo is a dome-shaped hill found in periglacial regions (Fig 147). They can be up to 60 metres high and 300 metres in diameter. Their exact formation is still a mystery. However, a lens of ice is always found at the core of a pingo and it seems likely that the expansion of water on freezing is an important process in their development (Fig 148).

Head

Head is the name given to the mixture of clay and angular rock fragments (Fig 149) which results from the process of solifluction (see page 28). It is a common deposit in the chalk regions of south-east England and with careful farming it can yield good crops.

Fig 147   A pingo

Fig 148   The possible formation of a pingo

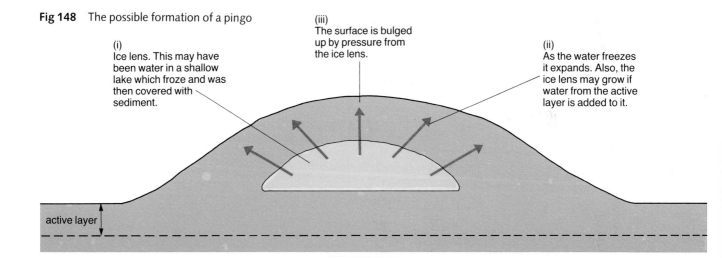

(i)
Ice lens. This may have been water in a shallow lake which froze and was then covered with sediment.

(iii)
The surface is bulged up by pressure from the ice lens.

(ii)
As the water freezes it expands. Also, the ice lens may grow if water from the active layer is added to it.

active layer

Loess

This is a wind-blown deposit of fine silt or dust. Loess is found in parts of Europe which experienced periglacial conditions during the Ice Age, such as northern France. This is because there was little or no vegetation to hold the surface together so the winds blowing out from the ice sheets were able to erode the soil and deposit it when they ran out of energy. Loess drains well and it is very fertile.

ENQUIRY

1   Copy Fig 145. Add labels to explain the formation of an ice wedge.
2   Study Fig 148. Explain the possible formation of a pingo.
3   Compare 'head' and 'loess' under the following headings – formation; particle size; and fertility.

Fig 149   Head

Ice and people

There are many ways in which glacial environments influence human activities. Glacial erosion has brought advantages such as streams in hanging valleys which can be harnessed for hydro-electric power, or superb mountain scenery which attracts tourists. It has also brought disadvantages such as steep slopes which are difficult to farm. Glacial deposition has left fertile soils in some places but infertile soils in others – the character of farming in Denmark is a good example of this point (see Discover Human Geography). Some of these influences are shown in Fig 150.

(i)

(ii)

(iii)

(iv)

Fig 150   Glacial environments and human activity

The Periglacial Environment

The periglacial environment presents particular problems for human activity. The permafrost itself is one of the main hazards. The active layer makes foundations unstable. Similarly, the warmth from buildings melts the permafrost and leads to a loss of support.

Modern technology can, to an extent, overcome these problems but the price is high and there has to be a good reason for making the effort. The discovery of oil at Prudhoe Bay in north Alaska in 1968 presented such a challenge. The reserve was estimated to contain 9.6 billion barrels of crude oil – an enormous quantity – but Prudhoe Bay is north of the Arctic Circle and ice makes transport by tanker impossible for most of the year. The only way the oil could be exploited was by building a pipeline across Alaska to the port of Valdez on the warmer south coast from where it could be shipped to oil markets around the world.

This was easier said than done and there were more problems than just the permafrost to cope with:

● **Cold and darkness.** Temperatures can drop to as low as −60 degrees Celsius and because Prudhoe Bay is north of the Arctic Circle, for two months of the year the sun never rises. Working conditions are therefore very unpleasant and even the metal used to build the pipeline had to be tested to make sure it could stand up to the very cold temperatures.

● **Earthquakes.** The pipeline crosses areas liable to earthquakes and in these places special supports had to be built to stop it from breaking in two.

● **Permafrost.** When crude oil reaches the surface it is still at a very high temperature. If the pipeline had been built below ground the warmth from the oil would have melted the permafrost and this would have resulted in the pipeline sagging and breaking. Consequently, for half its length the pipeline had to be built above ground and in order to protect it from snow and ice it had to be covered with a 10 cm thick insulating jacket.

● **Animal migrations.** Caribou, the North American reindeer, presented a big problem because the pipeline cut across their migration route. In these areas the pipeline had to be built below ground even in permafrost. This required covering it with a refrigeration jacket (run by an electric motor) to stop the warm oil from melting the permafrost and removing the pipeline's support.

The pipeline was built by the Alyeska Pipeline Service Company (formed by 8 separate oil companies) at a cost of £4700 million. The oil field is currently producing 1.7 million barrels of oil per day although this figure is expected to fall in 1990.

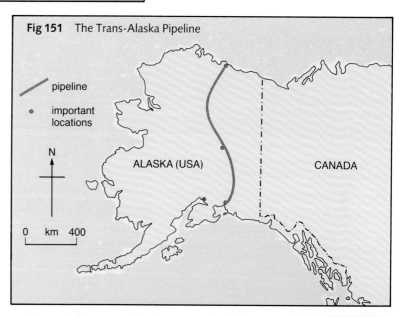

Fig 151   The Trans-Alaska Pipeline

— pipeline

● important locations

N

0   km   400

ALASKA (USA)

CANADA

Fig 152   Prudhoe Bay

Fig 153   Trans-Alaska Pipeline

ENQUIRY

1   Mention briefly some of the ways in which glaciers have a) helped and b) hindered human activity.

2   With the help of an atlas, mark the following onto a copy of Fig 151 – Prudhoe Bay; Fairbanks; Anchorage; Valdez; the Arctic Circle; the Brooks range; the Alaska Range; Mount McKinley; and the Yukon River.

3   How long is the Trans-Alaskan Pipeline?

4   How did periglacial conditions contribute towards the problems of building the pipeline?

5   Two problems are shown on your map but are not mentioned in the above account. What are they?

Glacial features on O.S. maps

Scale 1:50 000

Ordnance Survey OS

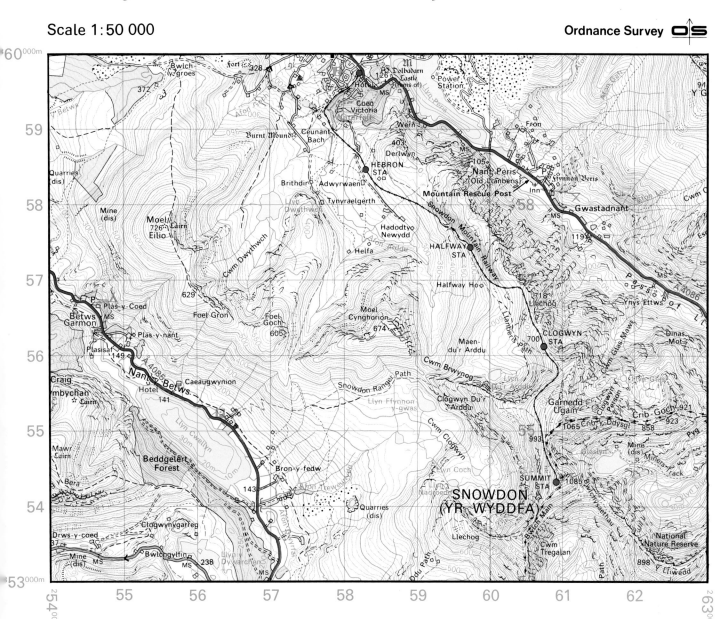

Fig 154

ENQUIRY

1 Name the glacial features found at the following Grid References on Fig 154:

a) Glasyln 617 546
b) Crib-goch 620 551
c) the summit of Snowdon 609 543
d) Llyn Cwellyn at 560 550
e) the valley at 547 547
f) the area of flat land between the main road and the lake in 56 54

2 Mark the above, and any other glacial features that you can identify, onto a tracing or sketch map of the extract.

3 Describe and comment on the relationship between relief, and roads and settlement.

4 What map evidence is there for past and present land-use?

THE SEA

How does the sea shape the land?

Waves

Most waves are the result of friction between the wind and the sea. However, it is important to remember that waves can be caused in other ways e.g. by submarine volcanic eruptions and/or earthquakes (see page 16).

The size of a wave depends on the strength of the wind, how long the wind has been blowing and the fetch – the amount of sea across which the wind has blown. The

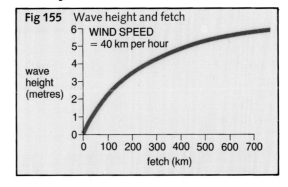

Fig 155 Wave height and fetch

Fig 156 Wave forms

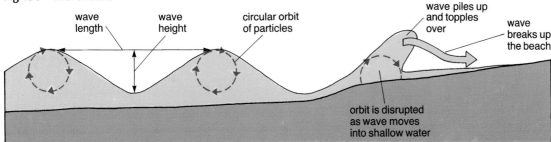

stronger the wind, the bigger the wave but it takes about 24 hours for waves to reach their maximum size and the fetch is a critical factor (Fig 155).

It is important to understand that it is the shape of the wave that moves forward, not the water itself. This explains why sea-gulls bob up and down on the waves without appearing to move. The wave is the way in which the energy transferred from the wind to the sea by friction is moved forward. As a complete wave passes a particular point each particle of water moves round in a circle. However, when a wave moves into shallow water the particles cannot complete their circle because they come into contact with the sea bed, and the height of the wave increases. Eventually, the wave breaks and topples over. The wave breaking up a beach is known as the swash. The water coming back down the beach is known as the back-wash (Fig 156).

Another change that happens as waves move into shallow water is that they slow down

and alter direction – a process known as wave refraction. If, for example, a wave is moving onto a coastline with a series of bays and headlands the section of the wave moving into the deeper water of the bay will move at a faster speed than the section of the wave moving into the shallow water off the headland. The result is that the wave front is bent as it moves into the bay and this has the further consequence of concentrating wave energy on the headlands (Figs 157 and 158).

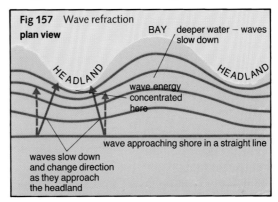

Fig 157 Wave refraction

Fig 158 Wave refraction in Lulworth Cove, Dorset

ENQUIRY

1 Describe and explain the relationship between wave height and fetch.
2 Explain why waves break when they move into shallow water.
3 Explain the difference between swash and backwash.
4 Sketch Fig 158. Make the wave refraction stand out clearly and label it.
5 Why is wave energy concentrated on headlands?

THE SEA

Coastal processes

1 Erosion

The same processes by which rivers wear away their valleys are the ways in which the sea wears away the coastline i.e. hydraulic action, abrasion, solution and attrition (see page 41). As a very rough guide if more than thirteen waves break on the coastline per minute, erosion is likely to be the main process.

2 Transportation

Tides and currents both move material. However, the most important process of transportation affecting the coastline is longshore drift. This is the process by which material is moved along a beach and it is the result of a combination of wave action and gravity (see Fig 159). In order to stop this movement of material wooden fences called groynes have been built across many of our beaches (Fig 160). This is done to protect the coast and/or to stop a valuable tourist attraction from being washed away!

3 Deposition

As with rivers and ice, deposition takes place when the sea lacks the energy with which to transport its load. Again, as a very rough guide if less than eight waves break on the coastline per minute, deposition is likely to be the main process.

Fig 159 Longshore drift

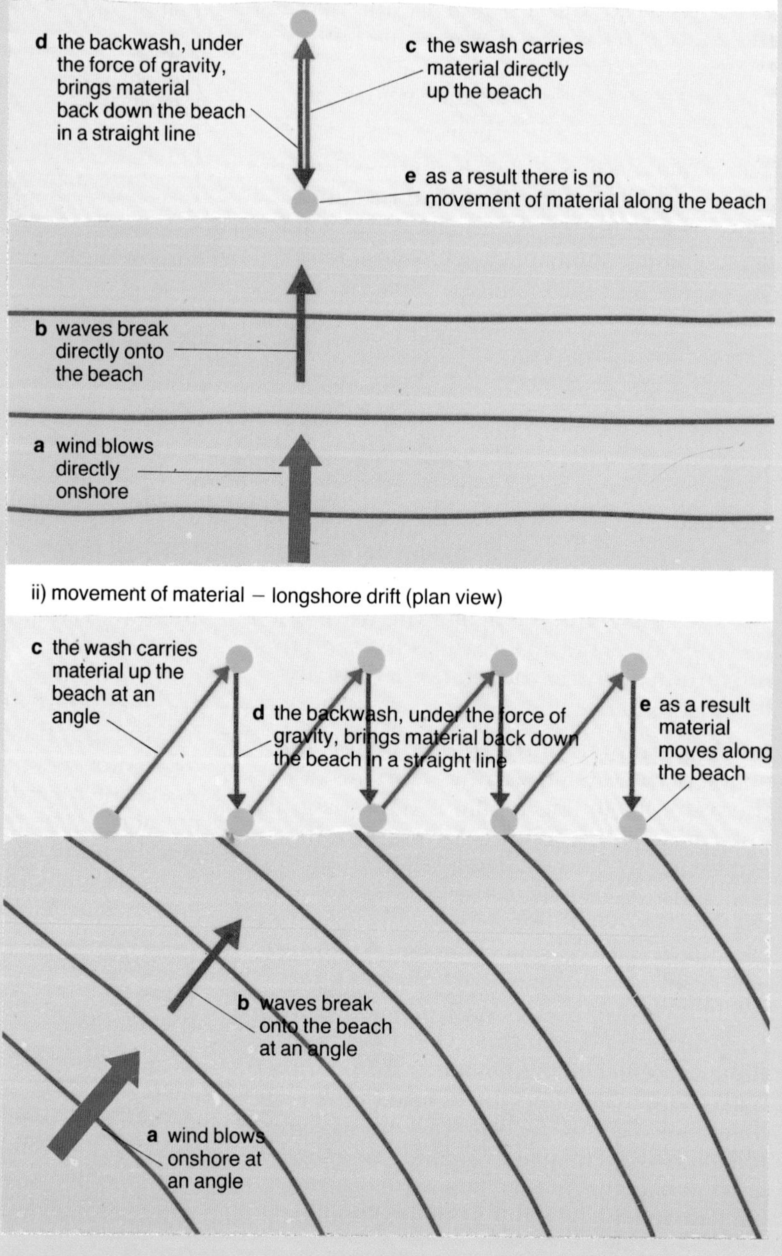

i) no movement of material (plan view)

d the backwash, under the force of gravity, brings material back down the beach in a straight line

c the swash carries material directly up the beach

e as a result there is no movement of material along the beach

b waves break directly onto the beach

a wind blows directly onshore

ii) movement of material — longshore drift (plan view)

c the wash carries material up the beach at an angle

d the backwash, under the force of gravity, brings material back down the beach in a straight line

e as a result material moves along the beach

b waves break onto the beach at an angle

a wind blows onshore at an angle

ENQUIRY

1 Which of the processes mentioned above do you think could be more important for coastal erosion than for river erosion, and why?
2 Explain, in detail, the process of longshore drift.
3 Why can the 'more than thirteen, less than eight' rule only be a very rough guide?

Fig 160
Beach with groynes

Features of coastal erosion

Cliffs and Wave-cut Platforms

Cliffs form where the sea is eroding an area of high land. The power of the sea is concentrated between the high and low water marks. A notch develops and when the overhang becomes too great the land above collapses. In this way the cliff retreats. The area of rock in front of the cliff (which used to be underneath the cliff before it was eroded backwards) is known as the wave-cut platform.

The shape of the cliff depends on a number of factors. Rapid erosion is more likely to produce a steep cliff because slow erosion allows time for weathering and mass movement to take place. Hard rocks are more likely to maintain a steep cliff while soft rocks are more likely to slump and collapse. The dip of the beds of rock also affects the steepness of a cliff; for example, if they are dipping towards the sea the cliff will probably slope at the same angle.

Many of the points discussed above are shown in Fig 161 (i)–(iv).

Fig 161
Cliffs and wave-cut platforms

(i) gentle profile in soft rocks being slowly eroded

(ii) profile controlled by dip of strata

(iii) cross section

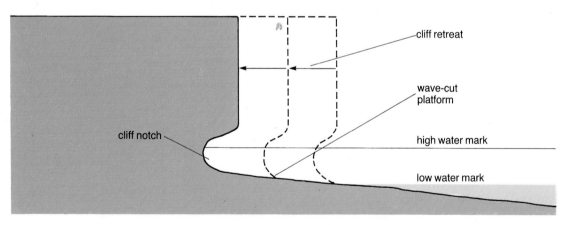

cliff retreat

wave-cut platform

high water mark

low water mark

cliff notch

ENQUIRY

1 With the aid of a labelled diagram only explain the formation of cliffs and wave-cut platforms.
2 Explain how each of the following factors is likely to affect the shape of a cliff – speed of erosion, rock type, rock structure.

(iv) steep cliffs with wave-cut platforms – the Kimmeridge Ledges, Dorset

Bays and Headlands

A bay is an opening in the coastline. A headland is a stretch of high land jutting out into the sea. They form because the sea erodes some parts of a coastline more quickly than others, usually because the rocks which make up the coastline are of different hardnesses.

If the bands of rocks are at or near right angles to the sea the coastline is described as being discordant. This arrangement of rocks makes it very easy for the sea to develop a series of bays and headlands because there is nothing to stop it attacking softer bands of rock which it erodes more quickly than any harder bands of rock e.g. Swanage Bay (Fig 162).

However, if the rocks are parallel to the sea (= a concordant coastline) a hard band of rock can protect a soft band of rock and this makes the sea's job much more difficult.

Bays and headlands can still form, though. This has happened on the Dorset coastline in the Lulworth Cove area (Fig 163). Stair Hole represents Stage 1 where the sea has managed to break through the hard limestones, perhaps by eroding along the line of a joint or fault (Fig 164). It is then able to wear away the soft Wealden Clays. The result is Stage 2, a bay lined up against the next hard band of rock, which is represented by Lulworth Cove (see also Fig 158, page 69). Stage 3 in the development of a concordant coastline is represented by the 'double bay' formed by the erosion of the headland which used to separate Man o' War Cove and St Oswald's Bay (Fig 165).

Fig 162　Swanage Bay, Dorset

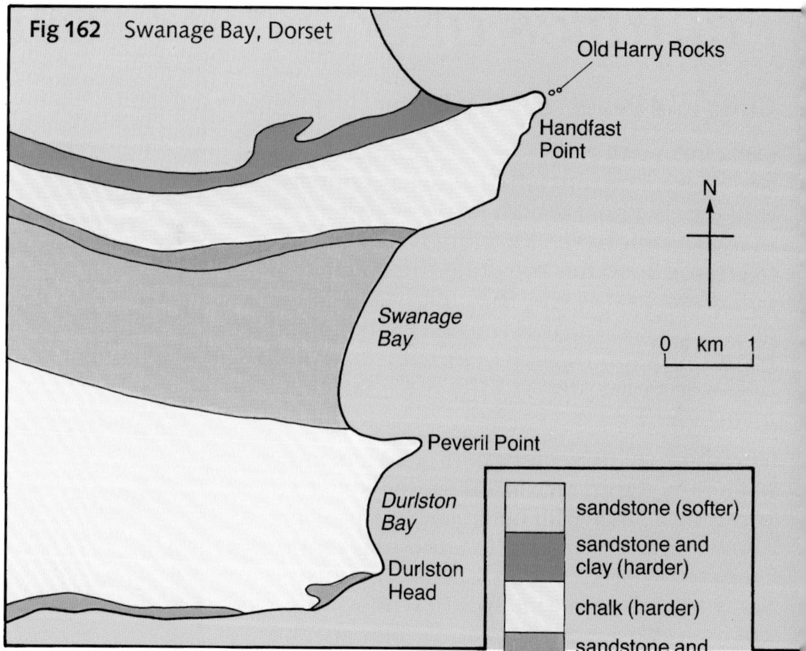

key:
- sandstone (softer)
- sandstone and clay (harder)
- chalk (harder)
- sandstone and clay (harder)
- clay (softer)
- limestone (harder)
- limestone (harder)

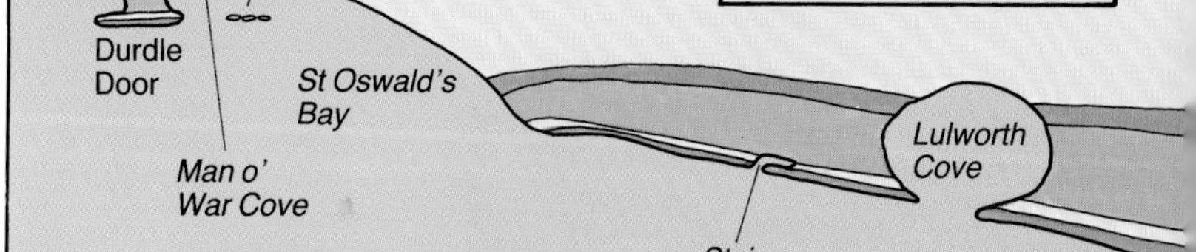

Fig 163　The development of bays and headlands on a concordant coastline

ENQUIRY

1　What is the main difference between a discordant and a concordant coastline?

2　Explain why Swanage Bay has formed.

3　Using labelled diagrams only, explain the development of bays and headlands on a concordant coastline.

4　If the sea has enough energy left, what do you think Stage 4 in the development of a concordant coastline could be?

Fig 164　Stair Hole

Fig 165　St Oswalds Bay

The Erosion of a Headland

Although headlands are areas of relatively hard rock they are exposed to wave attack on three sides and, as we have already seen (page 69), wave energy is concentrated on them. As a result headlands (like the one between Man o' War Cove and St Oswald's Bay, Figs 163 and 165) are themselves eventually eroded away.

Again, this happens in stages with the sea picking on areas of weakness first. A typical sequence is shown in Fig 166. Firstly, a joint or fault is eroded to form a cave. Sometimes a weakness extends vertically through a headland and water rushing into a cave may escape through such an opening which is known as a blowhole or gloup. If the cave wears right through the headland, the result is a natural arch. The roof of the arch is then attacked – from below by the sea and from above by the agents of weathering – until it eventually becomes so thin that it collapses. This leaves an isolated pillar of rock known as a stack. The stack itself is then undercut by the sea. It eventually collapses leaving a stump which is only exposed at low tide.

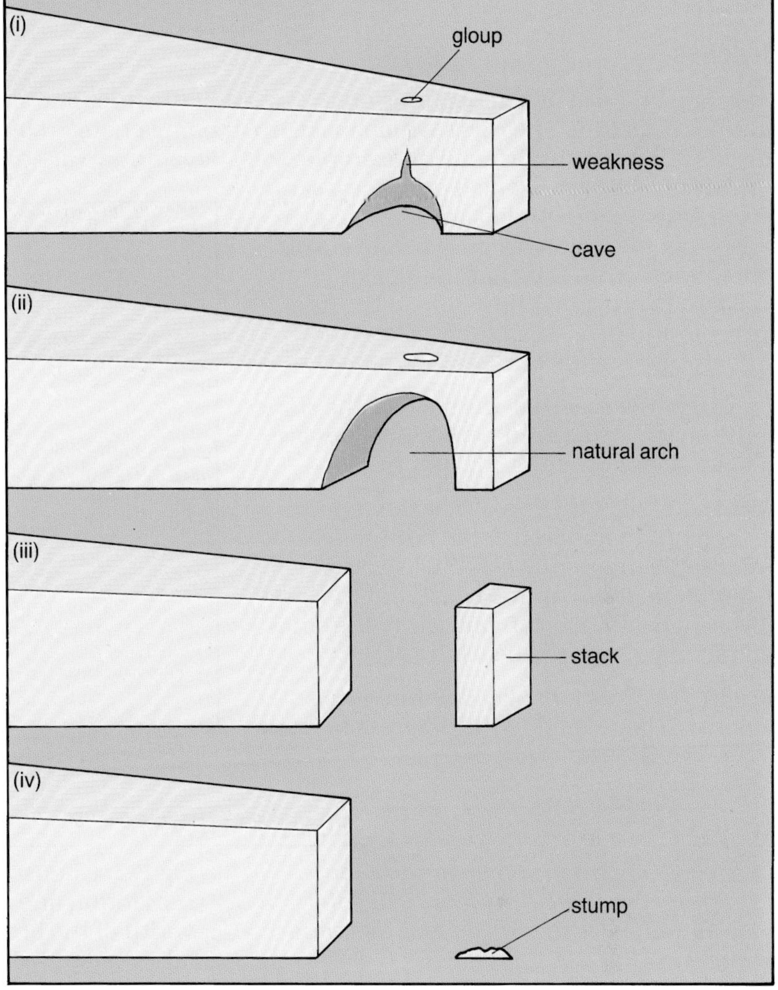

ENQUIRY

1   Make a sketch of Fig 167. Identify the following features – cliff; wave-cut platform; cove; natural arch and stack. Label these features and add brief definitions/explanations.

Fig 166   The erosion of a headland

(i)
gloup
weakness
cave

(ii)
natural arch

(iii)
stack

(iv)
stump

Fig 167   Old Harry Rocks

Features of coastal deposition

Beaches

The character of a beach depends on a number of factors. The rocks which make up the coastline are important. For example, soft sandstone cliffs are likely to produce a sandy beach whereas chalk cliffs are likely to produce a pebble beach because the layers of flint found within the chalk (see page 89) are resistant to erosion. The action of the tides, currents and processes such as longshore drift are also significant.

The larger the material, the steeper the slope of the beach. As a result pebble beaches are usually steeper than sandy beaches.

Also, material at the top of a beach tends to be larger than material at the bottom. This is because the more powerful swash is able to throw all material up the beach but the less powerful backwash can only carry the smaller material down the beach.

Beaches may also display different levels which can be related to the different heights of the tide. The shape of a beach is constantly being changed by the sea and the number of levels may vary during the course of a year.

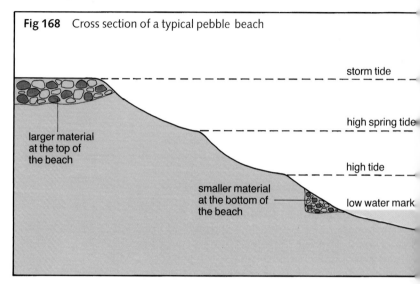

Fig 168   Cross section of a typical pebble beach

larger material at the top of the beach

smaller material at the bottom of the beach

storm tide

high spring tide

high tide

low water mark

BEACH SURVEYS

Beaches offer many opportunities for simple geographical projects. The following survey tests two ideas at the same time.

Aim   To test the ideas that:
1   Beaches have different levels.
2   Material at the top of a beach is larger than the material at the bottom.

Equipment   Tape measure. Meter rule. Ruler. Clinometer or spirit level.

Method
1   Stretch the tape measure across the beach. Use the clinometer or spirit level to keep the tape measure horizontal. Measure the difference in height between the tape measure and the surface of the beach at ½ metre intervals. If the beach falls away steeply it will be necessary to drop the tape measure and to add on the height dropped each time (Fig 169).
2   Measure the long axis of the pebble directly underneath the tape measure at each ½ metre interval.
3   Record your results in a table like the one in Fig 171.

Presentation of Results
1   Presenting the results is easy because of the way you have collected the information. An example is shown in Fig 172. Choose a suitable scale for the horizontal line which represents the width of the beach. The vertical scale allows you to show the difference in height between the tape measure and the surface of the beach. When you join the points up the beach levels should stand out.
2   A scatter graph is the best way to show this information (Fig 173). The horizontal axis represents the width of the beach and the vertical axis represents the diameter of the pebbles. If there is a trend, it should stand out.

Interpretation and Explanation
●   Were there different beach levels? If yes, how many and why? If no, why not?
●   Was material at the top of the beach larger than material at the bottom? If yes, why? If no, why not?

Conclusions   Briefly return to the ideas at the start of the survey. Have they been proved or disproved for the beach you have been studying?

Limitations   Did you have any problems when you carried out the survey? Were there any local factors which might limit the value of your results e.g. disturbance of the beach by tourists?

Fig 169 Measuring beach levels

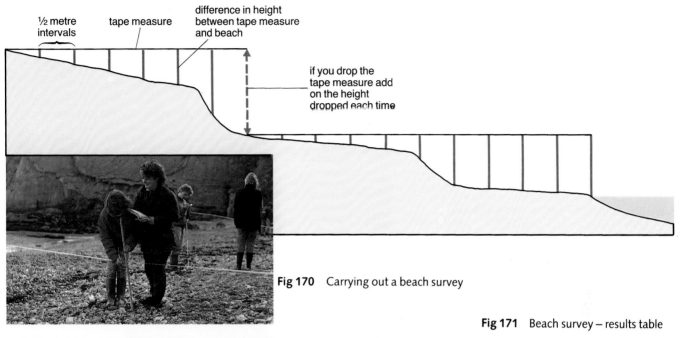

Fig 170 Carrying out a beach survey

Fig 171 Beach survey – results table

Distance from top of beach (metres)	0.0	0.5	1.0	1.5	2.0	2.5	3.0	3.5	4.0	4.5	5.0	5.5	6.0	6.5	7.0	7.5
Height from measure to beach (metres)	0.0	0.2	0.4	0.5	0.5	0.6	0.6	1.0	1.1	1.2	1.2	1.6	1.7	1.8	1.8	1.8
Long axis of pebble (centimetres)	18	15	20	14	13	14	11	10	2	9	7	10	5	1	1	2

N.B. These results are plotted in Figs 172 and 173.

Fig 172 Plotting beach levels

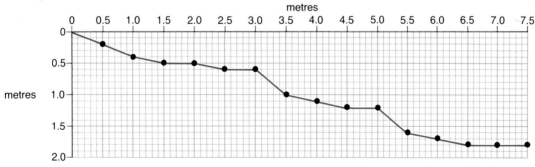

Fig 173 Plotting pebble size

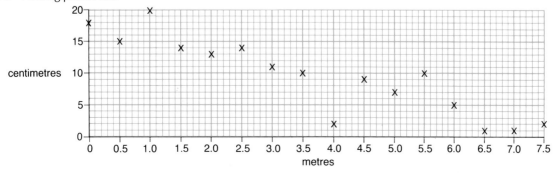

Spits

A spit is a beach extending out into the sea (Fig 174). Spits form only under certain conditions – longshore drift must be operating on the beach; there must be a sudden change in the direction of the coastline; the sea must be relatively shallow; and currents must be gentle.

Many spits are curved at one end by the action of the waves. These are known as hooked spits and Dawlish Warren in Devon is an example (Fig 175).

Sometimes, a spit may grow right across the mouth of a bay. These spits are known as bay-bars or barrier beaches and Slapton Sands in Devon is an example (Fig 176).

Occasionally, a spit may link the mainland to an island. Such a spit is known as a tombolo and a famous example is Chesil Beach which links the Dorset mainland to the Isle of Portland (Fig 177).

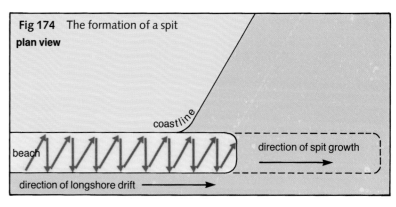

Fig 174   The formation of a spit

plan view

coastline

beach   direction of spit growth

direction of longshore drift

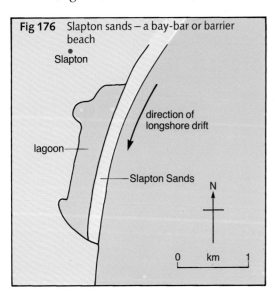

Fig 176   Slapton sands – a bay-bar or barrier beach

Slapton

direction of longshore drift

lagoon

Slapton Sands

N

0   km   1

Fig 175
Dawlish Warren, Devon

ENQUIRY

1   Explain why each of the conditions necessary for spit formation is important.

2   Draw and label a sketch or sketch map of each of the different types of spit mentioned on this page.

Fig 177
Chesil Beach – a tombolo

How do changes in sea-level affect the coastline?

We have already discussed some of the effects of changes in sea-level – for example, the formation of river terraces (page 49) and the creation of land bridges (page 53). However, such changes are bound to have a major effect on the coastline itself.

A Rise in Sea-level

A **fjord** is a glaciated valley which has been drowned by a rise in sea-level (see page 60). In contrast, a **ria** is an upland *river* valley which has been drowned by a rise in sea-level. Rias are therefore found in places where hills and river valleys which have not been glaciated meet the sea. There are many examples of rias in Devon, such as Salcombe (Fig 178).

If hills and valleys running parallel to the coastline are drowned by a rise in sea-level the result is a series of long, thin islands separated from the shore by narrow strips of water (Fig 179). This is known as a **Dalmatian coastline**. It is named after a region in Yugoslavia where an excellent example is to be found.

If the mouth of a lowland river valley is drowned by a rise in sea-level an **estuary** is formed (see page 49).

A Fall in Sea-level

There are some parts of the British Isles where the coastline shows evidence of a fall, rather than a rise, in sea-level. This is explained by the process of isostatic readjustment. During glacial periods the ice sheets were thickest in the north of the country. The tremendous weight of these ice sheets caused the land to sink slightly into the earth's crust.

When the ice sheets melted this enormous weight was removed and the land was able to recover, rising at the rate of a few millimetres a year. This recovery is still happening (Fig 180) and as a result there are places where the coastline is at a higher level than it was immediately after the Ice Age.

Fig 178   A ria – Salcombe, Devon

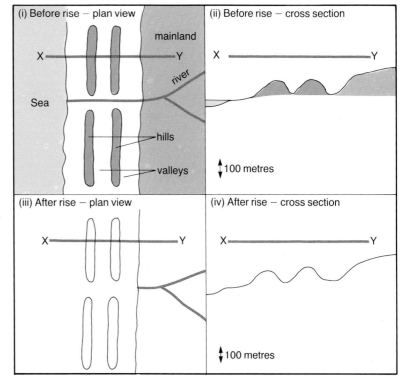

Fig 179   The formation of a Dalmatian coastline

Isostatic readjustment has made the north and the south of the country behave very much like the two ends of a see-saw. When the north sank, the south rose. Now that the north is rising the south is sinking and this is adding to the flood risk which has made schemes such as the Thames Barrage necessary (Fig 181).

A relative fall in sea-level can leave cliffs, beaches, wave-cut platforms and even stacks and stumps stranded above the present high water mark. Raised beaches and old cliff lines are a common feature on the west coast of Scotland (Fig 182).

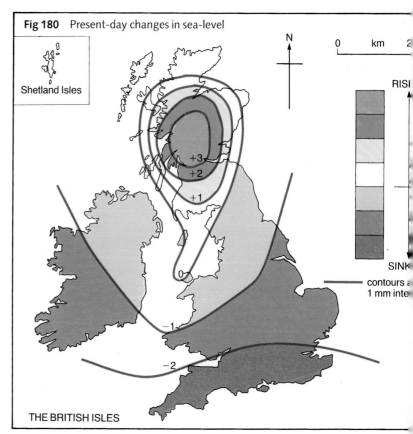

Fig 180   Present-day changes in sea-level

Shetland Isles

N

0   km   2

RISI

+3
+2
+1

0

−1

−2

SINK

contours
1 mm inte

THE BRITISH ISLES

Fig 181   The Thames Barrage

ENQUIRY

1   In what ways do you think the cross section of a ria will be different to that of a fjord, and why?

2   Compare a ria with an estuary under the following headings – appearance; formation; other features.

3   Re-draw Fig 179 to show what this section of coastline would look like after a 100 metre rise in sea-level.

4   Draw a sketch map of the Yugoslavian coastline from Rijeka in the north to Dubrovnik in the south. Add a suitable title and a brief explanation.

5   Which of these structures – concordant or discordant – is most likely to produce each of the following types of coastline – fjord; ria; Dalmatian?

6   Explain what is meant by the process of isostatic readjustment. How has this affected the coastline of the British Isles?

7   Make a sketch of Fig 182. Identify and label the raised beach and the old cliff line.

Fig 182   Raised beach with old cliff line

The sea and people

Many people's lives are directly or indirectly influenced by the sea. In some ways the sea offers opportunities while in other ways it threatens our activities. A few of the many themes you could follow up for yourselves are shown in Fig 183.

Fig 183   The sea and people

(i)

(ii)

(iii)

(iv)

TOURISM SURVEY

Some of you will live in a coastal resort. Many of you will visit one on holiday. Here is an idea for a Geographical Enquiry; data collection should take you no more than two days to complete.

Aim   To find out how facilities for tourists to _____ can be improved.

Method
1   Carry out a survey of the facilities currently offered for tourists and mark these onto a base map. Include all facilities from toilets to pony rides!
2   Check the main car parks at regular intervals throughout the day. Can they cope with the number of cars wanting to use them?
3   Carry out a questionnaire survey to find out what visitors think of facilities. Stick to two or three short questions. Try to interview at least ten young people, ten parents on holiday with their families and ten senior citizens.
4   Design another questionnaire for the people who run the tourist facilities e.g. the ice cream seller or the car park

attendant. Choose a quiet moment to interview at least five of them.
Carry out both of these surveys with a friend – not by yourself!

Presentation of Results   You should have no problems choosing a range of maps, graphs and tables to show your results.

Interpretation and Explanation   Describe the present facilities and attempt to explain their distribution. Describe and analyse the results of your car park survey and your questionnaire surveys. Did different age groups have different opinions? Did the tourists have different ideas to the people who worked there?

Conclusion   In what ways does your survey suggest that facilities for tourists can be improved. Where could these new facilities be located and why?

Limitations   Did you have any problems carrying out your survey? Are there any factors which might limit the value of your results?

DESERTS

Where are the world's deserts?

A desert is a place where all forms of precipitation (rain, snow, dew etc) are so low that very little, if anything, can grow. As a rough guide a desert gets less than 250 mm of rainfall a year. However, the balance between rainfall, run-off and evaporation is very important. For example, in some desert regions rainfall can be as much as 500 mm a year but run-off and evaporation are so high that very little of this water is available to support life.

Deserts can be divided into three types according to their temperatures –

- hot deserts (daytime temperatures as high as 50°C, night time temperatures as low as −10°C)
- temperate deserts (summer temperatures of around 20°C, winter temperatures of around −20°C)
- cold deserts (summer temperatures may barely reach 15°C while winter temperatures may fall to as low as −60°C)

The distribution of the world's deserts is shown in Fig 184. Some important factors help to explain this distribution.

The hot deserts are in tropical latitudes; they are in regions of high pressure which means that air is sinking and that rain is unlikely (see pages 101 and 105); and their predominate westerly winds blow across cold currents before reaching the land and as a result deposit most of their rain over the sea.

The temperate deserts are in mid latitudes; are in areas of high pressure; and are far inland, a long way from moisture bearing winds.

The cold deserts are in northerly latitudes; are in areas of high pressure; and have such low temperatures that the air can store very little moisture.

Fig 184 Distribution of the world's deserts

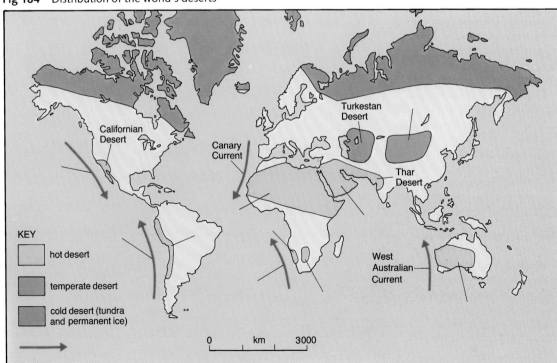

KEY

hot desert

temperate desert

cold desert (tundra and permanent ice)

Californian Desert

Canary Current

Turkestan Desert

Thar Desert

West Australian Current

0   km   3000

DESERTS

What shapes the land in the hot deserts?

1 Weathering

Weathering is a very important process in shaping desert scenery. Although the hot deserts are very dry, moisture is an important factor in the types of weathering which take place. The source of this moisture is mainly dew which forms at ground level during the cold desert nights.

Onion-skin weathering (exfoliation) has already been discussed (see page 23). A similar process is block disintegration. This happens when expansion during the hot desert day and contraction at night causes cracks to develop between the grains which make up the rock. This loosens the grains and if moisture gets into these cracks it further speeds up the rate of decomposition. Block disintegration is particularly common in rocks which are made up of a mixture of dark and light minerals. This is because the dark minerals have a lower albedo (see page 115) and therefore absorb more heat and, as a result, expand more than the light minerals.

The growth of salt crystals is another important type of weathering. Salt dust is blown into cracks by the wind. Moisture causes the salt crystals to expand. This exerts pressure on the rock and as a result it splits.

2 Water

Running water is another surprising agent in the formation of desert scenery. Firstly, it is important to remember that our climate has changed a great deal in recent geological time and many of the features we see in deserts began to form when the climate was wetter. Secondly, rain does fall in deserts, usually as heavy convection storms (see page 109) which may cause flash floods (see below). This water may last for only a short time but it can have a significant effect on the desert surface which is loose, unconsolidated and largely unprotected by vegetation.

Wadis

A wadi is a river channel in a desert which is usually dry (Fig 186). Wadis contain water only when there has been a desert storm, or rain or snow-melt in mountains many kilometres away. Violent desert downpours produce flash floods which have, for a short period of time, a tremendous amount of energy.

Fig 185 A desert landscape

Fig 186 Golden Canyon, a wadi in Death Valley, California

Isolated Hills

Isolated hills are a characteristic feature of many deserts. Various names have been used by geographers to describe them – inselbergs if they have rounded tops; mesas if they have flat tops; and buttes if they are a smaller version of mesas.

Until recently it was thought that inselbergs formed in a different way to mesas and buttes. However, new evidence suggests that all three features may well have a common origin. It seems likely that water begins the process by cutting steep sided canyons into the land surface. The landscape is then affected by weathering, wind erosion and further water erosion. The isolated hills we see today are all that is left of the former land surface (Fig 187).

The flat area of land surrounding these hills is known as a pediment.

Alluvial or Piedmont Fans

These fan-shaped deposits of material found where river channels leave the mountains to flow across the desert pediment are described and explained on page 48.

Playa

A playa is an old clay lake bed. Playa lakes may fill with water after heavy rain but they soon dry out. Salt is left behind by the evaporating water and the playa cracks and bakes hard (Fig 188).

Salt Pinnacles

It is hard to believe that 2 000 years ago a lake 9 metres deep filled Death Valley in California. The evaporating waters left a layer of salt 1.5 metres thick. Rain has dissolved the salt into the pinnacles you can see in Fig 189. Water drawn to the surface by the high temperatures evaporates and adds further deposits of salt to the pinnacles.

Fig 187   Isolated desert hills – The Olgas, central Australia

Fig 188   Playa

Fig 189   Salt pinnacles

ENQUIRY

1   Explain how water is important to the process of weathering in hot deserts.

2   Draw simple sketches of Figs 186, 187, 188 and 189. Give each sketch a suitable title and add notes to explain how the feature forms.

3 Wind

Deflation Hollows

These hollows vary in size from a few metres across to the huge Qattara Depression which is over 100 metres deep in places (Fig 190). They form when moisture collects in a small depression. This results in chemical weathering, with the wind removing the decomposed material. This allows more moisture to collect and the process repeats itself. The deflation hollow will stop growing when it is deep enough to protect the weathered material from the wind.

Mushroom Rocks

Mushroom rocks (Fig 191) are mainly the result of undercutting by wind-blown sand. Erosion is concentrated towards the base of the pillar because the wind cannot lift sand particles far above the surface. However, weathering is also important to this process because dew is most likely to occur at or near the ground surface. As a result, the base of these pillars is the zone of greatest chemical weathering.

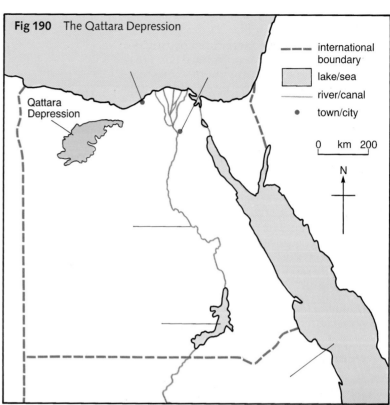

Fig 190 The Qattara Depression

- - - international boundary

lake/sea

river/canal

• town/city

0 km 200

N

Qattara Depression

Fig 191 Mushroom rock

Yardangs

These are long grooves separated by ridges of rock cut by wind-blown sand (Fig 192). They lie parallel to each other in the direction of the dominant wind.

Sand Dunes

We tend to imagine that hot deserts are a vast sea of sand. In fact, sand covers only a small proportion of the desert surface; for example, only a quarter of the Sahara Desert is sand while nearly half of it is mountain and nearly a quarter of it is bare rock or salt crust.

However, sand dunes are an important and often spectacular desert feature. They form when sand piles up against an obstacle, such as a boulder, and the largest dunes, known as **draas**, can reach a height of some 300 metres.

It is convenient to divide sand dunes into three different types. Ordinary sand dunes are rarely more than 30 metres high. They change shape with the wind, move irregularly and are usually found in swarms (Fig 193).

Fig 192   Yardangs

Fig 193   Ordinary sand dunes

Barchans are much less common. These are crescent-shaped dunes which vary between 2 and 30 metres in height and 20 to 200 metres in width and breadth. They form when the wind is always from the same direction. As the wind blows sand particles over the hump of the dune, it migrates downwind; speeds of up to 20 metres a year have been recorded. The curved horns are the result of sand being blown around the side of the dune.

Seif dunes are ridges of sand up to 200 metres in height and, in southern Iran, up to 100 kilometres in length. Their formation is far from certain but it has been suggested that they are the result of barchans being affected by a seasonal wind from another direction (Fig 195).

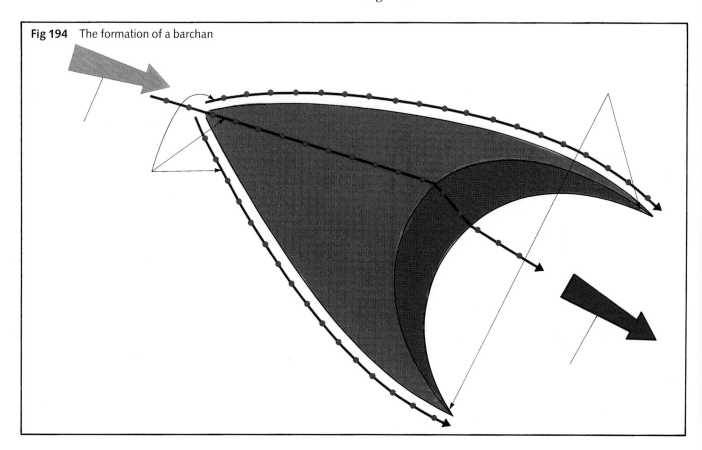

Fig 194   The formation of a barchan

ENQUIRY

1   Copy and complete the map of the Qattara Depression. Work out the approximate area of the Depression in square kilometres.
2   Sketch the photographs of the mushroom rock and the yardangs and add explanatory labels.
3   When and how do sand dunes begin to form?
4   Make a copy of Fig 194. Complete the labels to explain the formation of a barchan.
5   Describe and explain the possible formation of a seif dune.

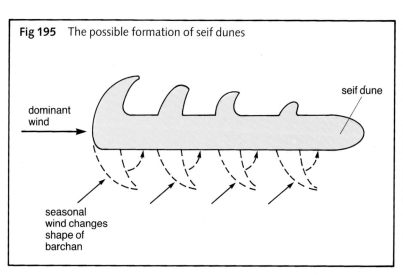

Fig 195   The possible formation of seif dunes

seif dune

dominant wind

seasonal wind changes shape of barchan

People and the hot deserts

The hot deserts are one of the most hostile environments on earth. In the past, permanent settlement has been possible only at an oasis or next to a river. Only nomads, such as the Bedouin of Arabia, have learnt to survive in the desert itself by moving from one water hole to the next, and theirs is a fast disappearing life-style.

However, given water the desert will flourish. Irrigation projects using traditional, simple technologies and modern, advanced technologies are discussed in *Discover Human Geography*. These schemes have brought many benefits as well as some problems.

One of the most spectacular recent examples of bringing the desert to life is that of agricultural development in Saudi Arabia. Between 1980 and 1985 US$20 billion was spent on irrigation. Between 1981 and 1984 the Saudi wheat harvest increased from 85 000 tons to 1.3 million tons. Most remarkable of all has been the development of the dairy and poultry sectors of the economy. Saudi dairy cattle can shelter from the sun under canopies which spray water at regular intervals and which are fitted with high speed fans (Fig 196)!

However, even this development has its cost, apart from the financial one. There is increasing concern about the lowering of the water table and the risk of salination. Also, the Saudi government is concerned as to whether or not the benefits are reaching the people they wanted to help most – the traditional rural population.

Fig 196 Stall fed Friesans, Saudi Arabia

ROCKS AND SCENERY

How do rocks affect the landscape?

In Section 1 we looked at various characteristics of the rocks which make up the earth's crust. In Sections 2 to 6 we considered the processes which shape these rocks into the scenery we can see around us. These processes are very important but the influence of the rocks themselves must not be forgotten. Some rocks are associated with their own special scenery and in this Section, three of these rocks will be considered in detail – chalk, Carboniferous Limestone and granite. The distribution of these rocks in the British Isles is shown in Fig 197.

Chalk

Chalk is a white, fine-grained limestone (Fig 198). It was deposited during the Upper Cretaceous period of geological time which lasted from 95 million to 65 million years ago. It is made up almost entirely of the protective plates of microscopic sea creatures kown as coccoliths. This means that chalk is almost pure calcium carbonate, although it may contain bands of flint (silica) formed, perhaps, from the remains of larger sea creatures (Fig 199).

Chalk is a porous rock which means that water can sink into it through spaces found between the fragments which make up the rock. It has a small number of joints and bedding planes, and water can also make its way along these, so chalk is also pervious.

Like all limestones, chalk dissolves in rain water (see page 24).

Fig 197　The distribution of chalk, Carboniferous limestone and granite in the British Isles

granites and similar rocks

carboniferous limestone

chalk

N

0　km　200

Fig 198 Chalk, with the fossil of a sea-urchin

Fig 199 Flint

ROCKS AND SCENERY

Chalk Scenery

Cuestas (Escarpments)   A cuesta is a bed of rock which has been tilted. It has one steep slope (the scarp slope) and one gentle slope (the dip slope) (Fig 200). Many rocks form cuestas but some of the best examples are to be found in areas of chalk such as the North and South Downs. This is because these areas have been gently tilted by earth movements and also because the chalk is able to maintain steep slopes.

Springs   Underneath the chalk are deposits of clay which is impermeable. As a result springs are often found at the junction between the two types of rock.

Dry valleys   Dry valleys are another common feature of chalk landscapes (Fig 201). For most of the year any surface water quickly sinks into the rock although in wet weather when the water table is high small streams, known as bournes, may flow briefly.

This leaves us with the problem of trying to explain how and when these dry valleys formed. One idea is that they were cut by rivers when our climate was much wetter. Another possibility is that they formed during the Ice Age when the ground was frozen. This would have made the chalk impermeable so water would have flowed across the surface instead of sinking in.

Chalk soils are thin and naturally infertile. The steeper scarp slopes are used mainly for sheep grazing although many of the gentler dip slopes have been improved with fertilisers and are used for arable crops, particularly barley. In some places chalk is quarried as a raw material for cement works.

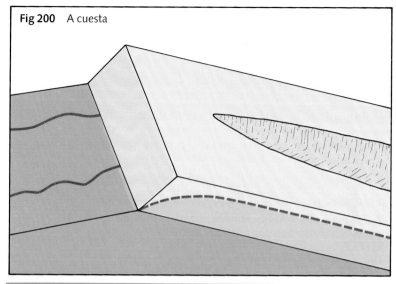

Fig 200   A cuesta

ENQUIRY

1   Show on a base map of the British Isles the distribution of chalk, Carboniferous Limestone and granite. With the help of an atlas label the following places:
– North Downs   – The Pennines
– South Downs   – The Cairngorms
– Salisbury Plain   – Central Ireland
– Chilterns   – Dartmoor
– Lincoln Wolds   – and Bodmin Moor.

2   Which group of rocks does chalk belong to, and why (see page 7)? Describe and explain how chalk forms.
3   Label the following features onto a copy of Fig 200 – scarp slope; dip slope; dry valley; spring; water table; sheep grazing; arable crops.
4   Explain how and when dry valleys may have formed.

Fig 201   Dry valley

Carboniferous Limestone

Carboniferous Limestone is a hard, grey shelly limestone. It was deposited during the Lower Carboniferous period of geological time which lasted from 370 to 325 million years ago. It is formed largely from the remains of crinoids, corals and brachipods (Fig 202). It is broken up by a regular pattern of joints and bedding planes.

Carboniferous Limestone is pervious but not porous. This means that water can only pass through it along its many joints and bedding planes.

Carboniferous Limestone Scenery

The characteristic features of Carboniferous Limestone scenery are to a large extent the result of the rock's colour, hardness and structure (jointing and bedding), and of its chemical reaction with rain water (see page 24). However, the following case study demonstrates that other factors are important as well.

In *Discover Human Geography* the problems of managing tourism, leisure and recreation in the Malham area of the Yorkshire Dales National Park were considered. One of the area's main attractions is the spectacular Carboniferous Limestone scenery; a walk of little more than 8 km takes you to examples of almost all the major features of this unique rock type (Fig 203).

Scars are steep, bare rock faces. They are common in areas of Carboniferous Limestone because of its hardness and blocky structure. Great Close Scar (Fig 204) marks the location of an east-west fault line. The land to the north has moved relatively upwards which helps to explain why Great Close Scar is such a prominent feature.

The permeable nature of Carboniferous Limestone means that surface water is unusual. Joints are enlarged by the process of solution (see page 41) until streams disappear down them. These depressions are known as **swallow holes**, sinks or pot-holes. The stream flowing southwards from Malham Tarn onto the Carboniferous limestone disappears down Water Sinks after only a few hundred metres (Fig 205).

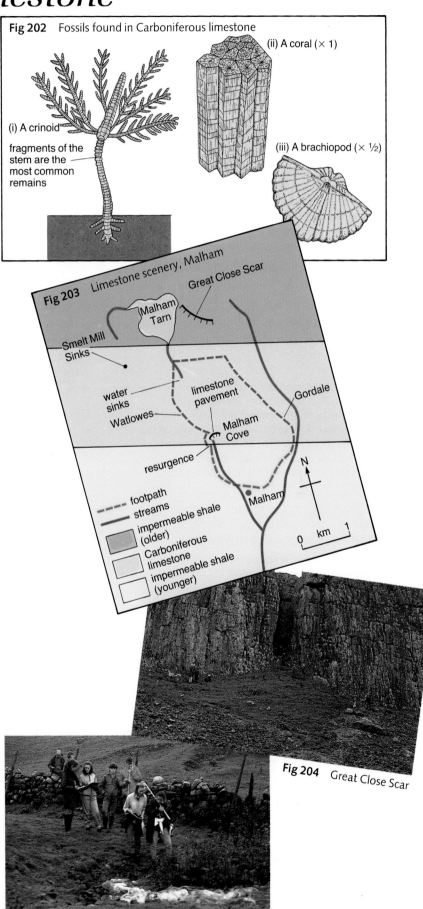

Fig 202   Fossils found in Carboniferous limestone

(i) A crinoid

fragments of the stem are the most common remains

(ii) A coral (× 1)

(iii) A brachiopod (× ½)

Fig 203   Limestone scenery, Malham

Great Close Scar

Malham Tarn

Smelt Mill Sinks

water sinks

limestone pavement

Gordale

Watlowes

Malham Cove

resurgence

N

footpath
streams
impermeable shale (older)
Carboniferous limestone
impermeable shale (younger)

Malham

0   km   1

Fig 204   Great Close Scar

Fig 205   Water sinks

The water continues to dissolve the limestone as it makes its way down through the system of joints and bedding planes. This can lead to the development of **underground caverns**. Stalagmites (which grow up from the floor), stalactites (which hang down from the roof) and pillars (which go from the floor to the roof) form when dripping water leaves behind tiny deposits of calcium carbonate (Fig 206).

Fig 206   Stalactites

The water eventually emerges as a spring, known as a **resurgence**, when the limestone meets an impermeable rock. However, the water may have taken a long and complicated route underground. For example, the resurgence at the base of Malham Cove comes from Smelt Mill Sinks and not, as you might think, from Water Sinks (Fig 207).

With so little surface water **dry valleys** are a common feature of Carboniferous Limestone scenery. Watlowes (Fig 208) is an excellent example. It probably formed when our climate was wetter or when the ice sheets were melting, in the same way that the dry valleys on chalk formed.

The south west facing slope of Watlowes (the sunnier side) is gentler than the north east facing slope (the shadier side) probably because it would have had greater temperature changes in periglacial times. As a result, freeze-thaw and solifluction processes (see pages 23 and 28) would have been more active.

Fig 207   Malham Beck flowing away from its resurgence

The magnificent dry stone wall was built in medieval times to separate the sheep of Fountains Abbey and Bolton Abbey.

Some gorges have small "misfit" streams in them e.g. Gordale (Fig 209). The steeper and occasionally overhanging sides of Gordale has led to the suggestion that it (like some other gorges in Carboniferous Limestone areas) might have formed when the roof of an underground cavern collapsed. However, it seems more likely that it formed like Watlowes when our climate was wetter, or when the ice sheets were melting.

Fig 208   Watlowes

Fig 209   Gordale

There are many examples of **limestone pavements** in the Malham area but the best one is at the top of Malham Cove (Fig 210). The blocks are known as clints and the gaps are known as grykes. The formation of limestone pavements is far from certain. Widening of the joints by solution is clearly an important part of the process but the bare rock surface is something of a mystery. One idea is that the soil was removed by an ice sheet. Alternatively, the soil may have been washed into the grykes as they became enlarged. A third idea is that deforestation by early man led to soil erosion and the exposure of the pavements.

The limestone soils of the Malham area are thin and stony and the main farm land-use is sheep grazing. In some places Carboniferous Limestone is quarried for building stone.

Fig 210   Limestone pavement, Malham Cove

(see page 7)

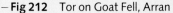

ENQUIRY

1   Which group of rocks does Carboniferous Limestone belong to, and why (see page 7)? Describe and explain how Carboniferous limestone forms.
2   Copy and complete Fig 211 by ticking the factors which help to explain each feature's formation and/or by writing in the appropriate information. Choose two of these features and with the aid of labelled sketches and/or diagrams explain in detail how they form.

Factor / Feature	Rock hardness	Rock structure	Chemical weathering	Glaciation/ Periglaciation	Other factors (please state)
Scars					
Swallow holes					
Caves, stalagmites etc.					
Resurgences					
Dry valleys/ gorges					
Limestone pavements					

Fig 211   Check list for limestone scenery

Granite

The characteristics of granite are described on page 6 and its reaction to chemical weathering is explained on page 24. It is an extremely hard, non-porous rock. It is largely impermeable but it does have some joints which formed when it cooled down and contracted; these mean that water is able to drain through it to a limited extent.

Granite Scenery

The granite areas of the British Isles are either mountains or moorland. In comparison with chalk and Carboniferous Limestone, granite has few special features. One difference is that there is surface drainage and streams have cut steep-sided valleys into the landscape. However, the most notable feature is the **tor** which is a mass of rocks found at the top of many granite hills (Fig 212).

— Fig 212   Tor on Goat Fell, Arran

How tors form is not certain. One suggestion is that they develop where joints are widely spaced because these places are less affected by weathering than places where joints are close together (Fig 213). However, present-day rates of weathering are too slow to produce such features so it seems likely that the tors we see today formed several millions of years ago when our climate was much warmer and when rates of weathering were much faster.

Granite landscapes are generally bleak, wet and wind-swept. Soils are thin and poorly drained. Extensive sheep grazing is the main farm land-use. In some places granite is quarried as building stone.

The granite intrusions of Cornwall are associated with deposits of tin and other valu-able metals. These formed the basis of an important mining industry but most of the mines have been worked out or are no longer economic. Cornwall also has deposits of kaolin (China clay). This is a white powder which forms when the feldspars in granite are decomposed by hot fluids from within the earth's crust. It is used to make porcelain and in the manufacture of paper. Kaolin is mined at Lee Moor on the edge of Dartmoor, and at St Austell Moor. It is hosed out of the quarries by high pressure water jets (Fig 214).

Granite areas have also been used for reservoirs because they have a low population density; are of low agricultural value; they have a high rainfall; the granite is suitable for dam construction; and it is largely impermeable.

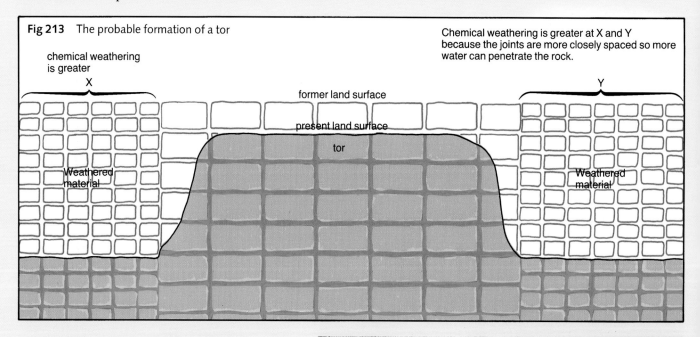

Fig 213 The probable formation of a tor

chemical weathering is greater

Chemical weathering is greater at X and Y because the joints are more closely spaced so more water can penetrate the rock.

X

former land surface

present land surface

tor

Weathered material

Y

Weathered material

ENQUIRY

1 Make a sketch of Fig 212. Explain how tors probably form.
2 What do you think are the main differences between granite, chalk and Carboniferous Limestone landscapes? Are there any similarities?
3 Read through this Section again. Explain the difference between permeable and impermeable; and porous and pervious.

Fig 214 A kaolin quarry

Rocks on O.S. maps

ENQUIRY

Fig 215 is a simple guide to rock spotting on O.S. maps. It can only give an indication and it has to be used with care. To be certain you would need to consult a geology map or, better still, to carry out your own fieldwork.

1   On the basis of map evidence only, what rock type(s) is/are shown on the extract, Fig 216? Explain your reasons in full.

2   Draw a sketch section along Easting 80. Label as many features of the physical and human environment as you can identify.

3   Describe and explain the distribution of roads and settlements on the extract.

Rock	Evidence	Rock	Evidence
Chalk	▪ little, if any, surface drainage ▪ cuestas (escarpments) ▪ springs ▪ dry valleys ▪ the place names coombe, bourne, down ▪ rarely higher than 350 metres	Carboniferous limestone	▪ little, if any, surface drainage ▪ scars ▪ pot holes, swallow holes, sinks, springs ▪ dry valleys ▪ the place names knoll, dale ▪ it may form upland areas as high as 700 metres
Granite	▪ surface drainage ▪ generally hilly, often with some steep slopes ▪ tors ▪ granite forms some very high areas e.g. up to 600 metres in Cornwall and over 1000 metres in Scotland	Clay	▪ surface drainage ▪ low hills, rarely more than 30 metres high

Fig 215   Rock spotting on OS Maps

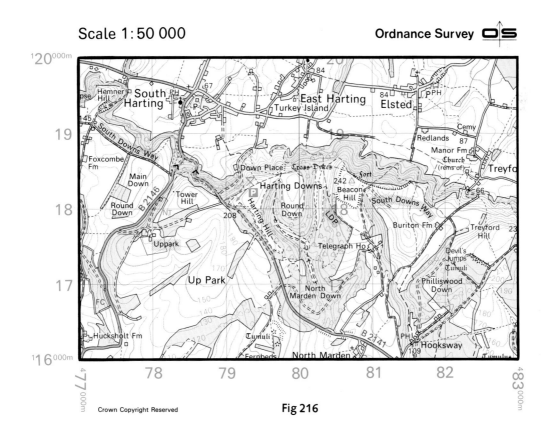

Scale 1:50 000   Ordnance Survey O**S**

Crown Copyright Reserved   **Fig 216**

WEATHER AND CLIMATE

What makes up the weather?

Weather means day to day conditions of temperature, wind etc whereas climate refers to general conditions. For example, the British Isles can have cold, rainy weather one day and warm, sunny weather the next; these day to day conditions are part of what makes up our temperate maritime climate (see page 114).

Fig 217 What makes up the weather?

1 Write down a list of all the things you can think of which make up the weather.

2 Re-write your list under the following headings – temperature; precipitation (this includes any form of water which reaches the ground e.g. rain, snow, dew); cloud; wind; others.

Measuring the weather

Accurate measurements are necessary so that we can describe, explain and hopefully predict the weather. There are many relatively simple weather instruments, a number of which are described on the following pages. The thermometers are kept in a Stevenson's Screen (Fig 218). This allows the air's temperature to be measured without it being affected by direct sunlight or wind.

The modern meteorologist can also collect data from advanced scientific instruments, such as weather satellites (Fig 219). However, if you wish to look for evidence of climatic change you need a long period of comparable records, so the days of the Stevenson's Screen are far from over!

Fig 218 Stevenson's screen

Fig 219 Satellite image

WEATHER AND CLIMATE

Measuring Temperature

Temperature is measured in degrees Celsius (°C). The two most important temperatures of the day are the maximum (the highest) and the minimum (the lowest). These can be recorded with a Six's Thermometer (Fig 220).

Measuring Humidity

Humidity is the amount of water vapour in the air. Warm air can hold more water vapour than cold air so it is more important to know the relative humidity of the air than the absolute humidity. When relative humidity reaches 100% the air is completely saturated and the water vapour condenses out to form clouds or rain etc.

Relative humidity can be measured with a hygrometer (Fig 221). This consists of a wet bulb and a dry bulb thermometer. The wet bulb is an ordinary thermometer with a piece of muslin tied round it which stays permanently wet because it is dipped into a container of water. The dry bulb is just an ordinary thermometer.

Water evaporates until air reaches its saturation point, and evaporation produces cooling. Therefore, water evaporates from the wet bulb until the air reaches its saturation point and the cooling means that the wet bulb shows a lower temperature than the dry bulb. When saturation point is reached there is no evaporation and no cooling so the thermometers record the same temperature. Thus, the difference in temperature between the two thermometers can be used to work out the relative humidity of the air.

Measuring Rain

Rainfall is measured with a rain gauge (Fig 222). This is a metal cylinder which contains a funnel and a collecting jar. Any rain which is collected is poured into a glass jar and measured in millimetres.

It is important to place a rain gauge in an open space away from trees and buildings and the top of the cylinder must be at least 30 cm above the ground in case of splashing.

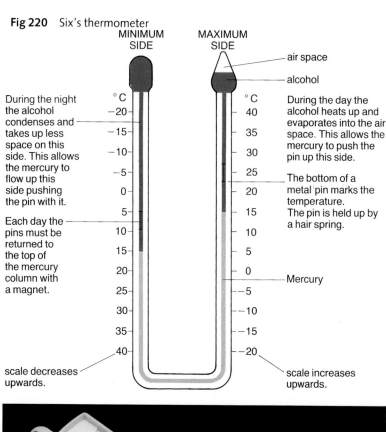

Fig 220 Six's thermometer

MINIMUM SIDE

MAXIMUM SIDE

air space

alcohol

During the night the alcohol condenses and takes up less space on this side. This allows the mercury to flow up this side pushing the pin with it.

Each day the pins must be returned to the top of the mercury column with a magnet.

°C (minimum)	°C (maximum)
−20	40
−15	35
−10	30
−5	25
0	20
5	15
10	10
15	5
20	0
25	−5
30	−10
35	−15
40	−20

During the day the alcohol heats up and evaporates into the air space. This allows the mercury to push the pin up this side.

The bottom of a metal pin marks the temperature. The pin is held up by a hair spring.

Mercury

scale decreases upwards.

scale increases upwards.

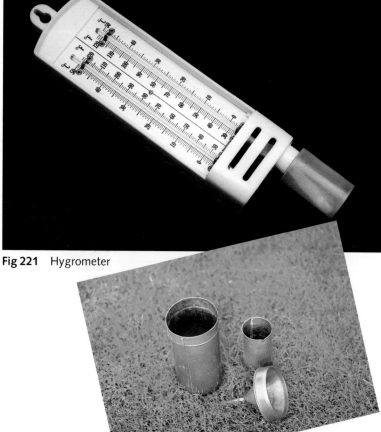

Fig 221 Hygrometer

Fig 222 Rain Gauge

Cloud Type

Clouds form when air is cooled and water vapour condenses out to form water droplets or ice particles. Clouds are put into groups mainly according to their shape and height. Some useful words to know are – cirrus (whispy clouds); cumulus (lumpy clouds); stratus (a layer cloud); nimbus (rain bearing); and alto (medium height). Some common cloud types are shown in Fig 223.

Cloud Cover

The amount of cloud covering the whole sky is estimated to the nearest eighth and shown with one of the symbols in Fig 224. An eighth of cloud cover is known as an okta, so, for example, ⅜ cloud cover is 3 oktas.

Fig 224   Cloud cover

amount of cloud (oktas)	symbol
0	◯
1	◔
2	◔
3	◑
4	◑
5	◕
6	◕
7	◕
8	●
sky obscured	⊗

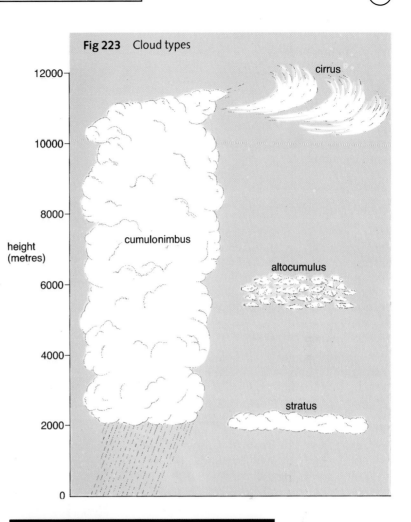

Fig 223   Cloud types

Measuring Sunshine

An instrument like the one in Fig 225 can be used to measure the amount of sunshine. The glass sphere focuses and concentrates the sun's rays onto a piece of card which is marked off in hours. When the sun shines the card is burnt and at the end of the day the time represented by the burnt sections can be added together to give the total amount of sunshine.

Measuring Wind Speed and Direction

Wind speed is measured with an anemometer. Ideally, this should be fixed to a post 10 metres above ground level but a hand held anemometer (Fig 226) gives useful and interesting results. The wind blows the cups round and the speed is read off a dial in miles, kilometres or knots per hour (a knot is a nautical mile which is 1.85 km). Speeds are recorded in kilometres per hour.

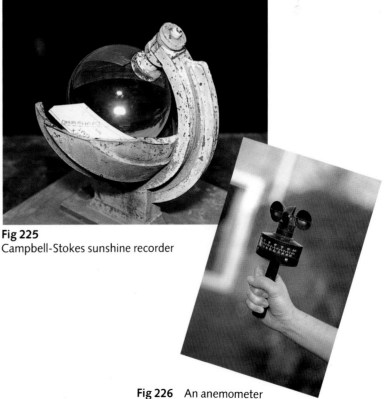

Fig 225
Campbell-Stokes sunshine recorder

Fig 226   An anemometer

Alternatively, wind speed can be estimated with the Beaufort Wind Scale. Some examples from this scale, which runs from 0 to 12, are given in Fig 227.

Wind direction is measured by a wind vane (Fig 228). The arrow always points in the direction from which the wind is coming, and this is the direction which gives the wind its name.

Measuring Atmospheric Pressure

Atmospheric pressure is the weight of air pressing down on the earth's surface. The easiest way to understand this is to think of a column of air above each of us extending upwards to the limit of the atmosphere. This column of air weighs a little over 1 kilogram per square centimetre. Fortunately, we have adapted to this weight so we do not notice it!

Atmospheric pressure is measured in millibars (mb). It can be recorded with a barometer, or a barograph like the one in Fig 229. It consists of a metal cylinder, the top of which flexes with changes in air pressure. The cylinder is connected by a series of levers to a pen. This rests on a piece of card attached to a drum which rotates once every 24 hours. A continuous record of pressure is marked onto the card as it moves under the pen.

Scale number	Wind description	How to spot it	Speed (km/hour)
2	light breeze	leaves rustle	6–11
4	moderate breeze	small branches sway	20–29
6	strong breeze	large branches sway	37–49
8	fresh gale	twigs break off trees	61–73
10	whole gale	trees are uprooted	87–100
12	hurricane	widespread devastation	121 and above

Fig 227   The Beaufort Wind Scale

Fig 228   Wind vane

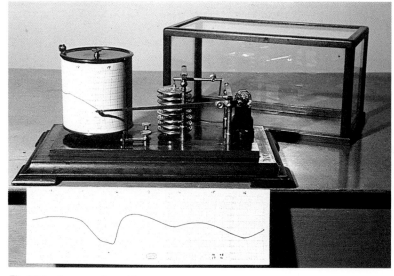

Fig 229   Barograph and barogram

Where does our weather come from, and why?

Air Masses

Weather in the British Isles is very change-able. This is because we can be affected by one of five main air masses (Fig 230). An air mass is a large body of air which has more or less the same characteristics throughout e.g. temperatures will be similar in all places covered by it.

The maritime air masses pick up moisture from the sea and as a result they bring wet weather. The continental air masses are dry because they cross only land and conse-quently pick up very little moisture. However, Polar Continental winds can bring snow showers in the winter because they pick up moisture when they cross the North Sea.

The polar and arctic air masses are generally colder than the tropical air masses. However, the continental interiors warm up in the summer and as a result the Polar Continental air mass brings hot weather with it.

Winds and Pressure

Air masses are brought to us by the wind which, in turn, is the result of differences in atmospheric pressure (Fig 231).

Warm air rises and expands. This means that the weight of air pressing down on the earth's surface is lighter. The result is an area of low pressure. In comparison, cool air sinks and contracts. This means that the weight of air pressing down on the earth's surface is heavier. The result is an area of high pressure.

The heavier air in the high pressure area is squeezed out towards the low pressure area – think of the air being squeezed out of a football. Wind is this movement of air from high to low pressure.

Of course, the system has to complete itself or we would run out of air. This happens at high altitude where rising air spills out to take the place of sinking air. As a result, high altitude winds blow in a different direction to low altitude winds. You can sometimes see this happening when there is cloud at two different levels.

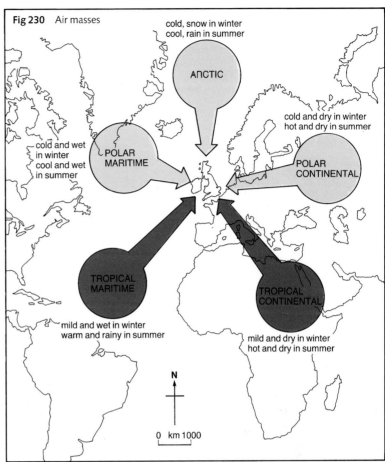

Fig 230　Air masses

cold, snow in winter
cool, rain in summer

ARCTIC

POLAR MARITIME
cold and wet in winter cool and wet in summer

POLAR CONTINENTAL
cold and dry in winter hot and dry in summer

TROPICAL MARITIME
mild and wet in winter warm and rainy in summer

TROPICAL CONTINENTAL
mild and dry in winter hot and dry in summer

N

0　km 1000

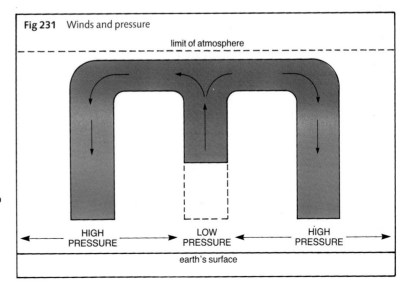

Fig 231　Winds and pressure

limit of atmosphere

HIGH PRESSURE　　LOW PRESSURE　　HIGH PRESSURE

earth's surface

Isobars

Isobars are lines drawn on weather maps which join places of equal pressure corrected to sea-level (this correction is necessary because pressure decreases with height). Winds blow down the pressure gradient from higher to lower numbers i.e. from higher to lower pressure. The closer together are the isobars, the stronger is the wind.

However, the wind does not blow in a straight line from high to low pressure because of the west-east rotation of the earth.

Winds in the northern hemisphere are deflected to their right while winds in the southern hemisphere are deflected to their left.

In the northern hemisphere this means that winds will always blow out from a high pressure system in a clockwise direction and into a low pressure system in an anticlockwise direction (Fig 232). In the southern hemisphere this relationship is the other way round.

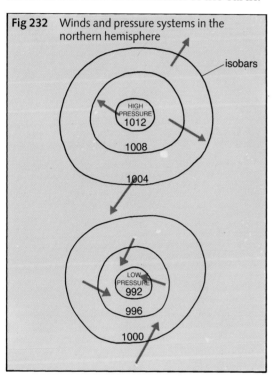

Fig 232   Winds and pressure systems in the northern hemisphere

Air Mass	Wind Direction	Winter Weather	Summer Weather
	North		
Polar Maritime			
		cold and dry; possible snow showers	
			warm and rainy
	South East		

Fig 233   Air masses – a check list

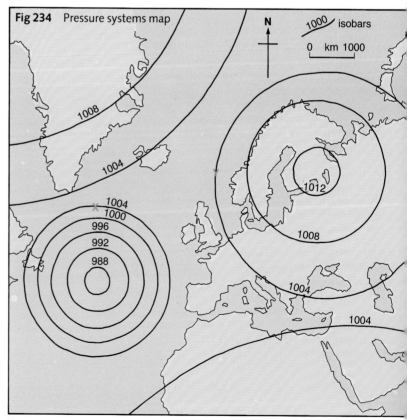

Fig 234   Pressure systems map

ENQUIRY

1   Copy and complete the table in Fig 233.
2   Copy Fig 231 and add labels to explain the causes of high pressure, low pressure and wind.
3   Label onto a copy of Fig 234:
– the centres of high and low pressure
– the approximate wind directions at places X and Y
– an area of relatively strong winds
– an area of relatively light winds
– and the name of the air mass affecting the British Isles.
What type of weather is this air mass probably bringing?

What is the weather forecast all about?

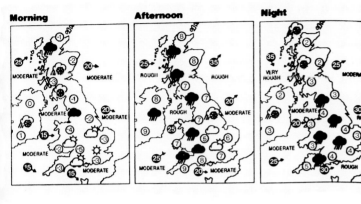

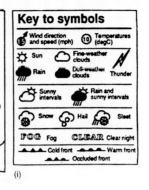

Fig 235 Newspaper forecasts

No radio or television news, or daily newspaper, is complete without a weather forecast. The weather is presented in many different ways – some examples are shown in Fig 235.

The official symbols used by the Meteorological Office are shown in Fig 236. A set of symbols is drawn for each weather station; an example is given in Fig 238. The scheme shown in Fig 224, page 99 is used to show cloud cover.

Region	Forecast
1	Morning – cold, temperatures below freezing to −3°C. Cloud in the west of the region, clear skies in the east. Afternoon – temperatures rising to a maximum of 7°C, becoming cloudy. Night – rain spreading into the region from the west with temperature dropping to 3°C. Winds westerly, increasing during the day up to 30 mph.
2	
3	
4	

Fig 237 (i) Weather forecast table   (ii) Weather forecast regions

WEATHER		WIND	
Symbol	Weather	symbol	wind speed (knots)
=	mist	◎	calm
≡	fog	⚲	1 – 2
,	drizzle	⚲	3 – 7
⁹	rain and drizzle	⚲	8 – 12
•	rain	⚲	13 – 17
✳	rain and snow		for each additional half-feather add 5 knots
✳	snow		
▽	rain shower	⚲	48 – 52
✳▽	rain and snow shower	**FRONTS**	
▽	snow shower	▬●●● warm	
⌂	hail shower	▬▲▲▲ cold	
R	thunderstorm	▬●▲● occluded	

Fig 236 Official weather symbols

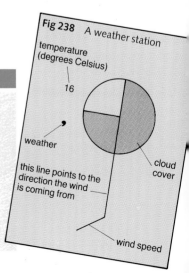

Fig 238 A weather station

ENQUIRY

1 Complete a copy of Fig 237 (i) by using the information given on the weather maps in Fig 235 (i). The regions are shown on Fig 237 (ii). The forecast for the first region has been done for you.

2 Choose a day to compare a weather forecast in your paper at home with what actually happens. Stick the weather forecast into your exercise book or folder along with your account. Did the forecasters get it right?

3 Describe the weather shown by the conventional symbols in Fig 238.

4 Draw symbols to show the following conditions recorded by a weather station: temperature = 12 degrees Celsius; rain; wind direction = south westerly; wind speed = 15 knots; cloud cover = ⁷⁄₈.

Fronts and Depressions

How many times have you heard the weather forecaster say that there is a warm front moving across the country, or that a depression will bring unsettled weather to all parts? If you haven't you won't have to listen to many forecasts before you do because fronts and depressions dominate much of our weather!

A front is a boundary between two air masses. Fronts are a common feature of our weather because the British Isles is often the meeting place for polar and tropical air masses.

The warm tropical air rises when it meets the cold polar air. This causes a bulge to develop in the front. The warm and cold fronts are the two sides of this bulge – the warm front marks the arrival of the tropical air and the cold front marks the arrival of the polar air. An occluded front is where the warm and cold fronts meet at the apex of the bulge (Fig 239).

Two other things happen as the warm air rises. Firstly, a low pressure system develops, and this is what is known as a depression. Secondly, the air cools down and water vapour condenses out to form clouds which eventually produce rain (see page 108).

Depressions move eastwards under the influence of the prevailing westerly winds. As they pass across the country each sector brings with it its own particular conditions (Fig 240) – this explains why our weather is so changeable! It is easy to forecast the approach of a depression because of the regular pattern of cloud types found along the warm front.

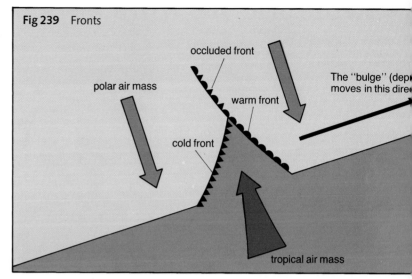

Fig 239 Fronts

occluded front

polar air mass

warm front

cold front

The "bulge" (dep⟩ moves in this dire⟨

tropical air mass

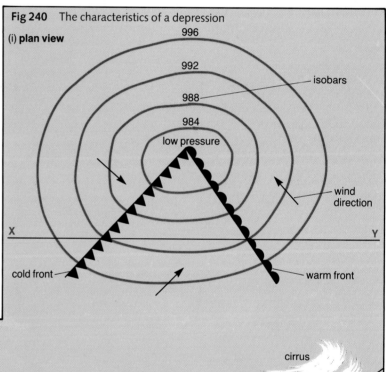

Fig 240 The characteristics of a depression

(i) **plan view**

996

992

988

984

low pressure

isobars

wind direction

X   Y

cold front

warm front

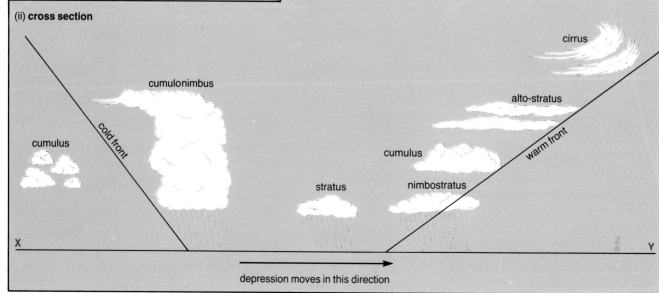

(ii) **cross section**

cirrus

cumulonimbus

alto-stratus

cumulus

cold front

cumulus

stratus

nimbostratus

warm front

X   Z   Y

depression moves in this direction

Jet Streams

The position of the front between the polar and tropical air masses, and therefore the path followed by depressions, varies. In the summer it tends to move northwards while in the winter it can move as far south as the Mediterranean.

This position is controlled by the polar jet stream which is a high altitude wind. It is found at about 9 km above the earth's surface and blows in an easterly direction with wind speeds of typically 100 km per hour, although they can reach 350 km per hour. It is itself a result of the collision between the giant polar and tropical air masses.

The jet stream follows a meandering course. However, the number of meanders varies between two and six. There are usually fewer in the winter when the air is moving faster.

Depressions always develop at the start of a poleward moving section of the jet stream and collapse when it begins to turn southwards. It is therefore easy to appreciate the effect the jet stream's position has on our weather.

Until we know more about the causes of the jet stream it will not be possible to predict its path for more than a short time into the future; and even when its pattern seems set it can change without warning.

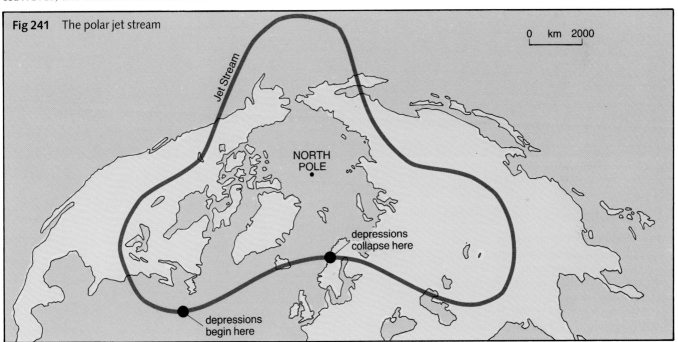

Fig 241   The polar jet stream

Anticyclones

Anticyclones are high pressure systems. Unlike depressions, they tend to remain stationary so they usually mean settled weather for several days. Isobars tend to be widely spaced so wind speeds are usually light.

High pressure systems are, of course, associated with sinking air. This means that clouds are unlikely to develop which makes fine, dry weather a characteristic feature of anticyclonic conditions. However, there are important differences depending on the season.

In the summer, anticyclones tend to bring sunny, dry, hot weather. However, the cloudless skies mean that heat rapidly escapes at night time. As a result, nights can be quite cool.

Later on in the year, this night time cooling can produce quite cold temperatures near the ground. When this happens water vapour condenses out to form mist or fog. The mist or fog persists until the heat of the sun the next day clears it.

In the winter, the weak sun means that day time temperatures tend to be low and the clear skies mean that night time temperatures are even lower. Typical days are therefore cold and bright and typical nights are dry but very cold and icy. If fog forms during the winter the sun is very often too weak to clear it. If it is very cold freezing fog and frost can form.

Fig 242 An autumn fog

1 What are fronts, and why are they a common feature of our weather?

2 What is a depression, and why do depressions form where the polar and tropical air masses meet?

3 Make a copy of Fig 240 (ii). Label the warm and cold sectors and the wind direction in each of these sectors (see Fig 240 (i)). Describe how the weather would change at place Z as the depression passes over.

4 What is the polar jet stream and why is it important?

5 Would the British Isles be affected by depressions if the conditions in Fig 241 existed? Explain your answer.

6 What is an anticyclone?

7 Why are depressions, but not anticyclones, associated with rain?

8 Copy and complete Fig 243 which compares anticyclonic conditions in summer and winter.

9 Explain why anticyclones are often associated with mist and fog.

	Summer	Winter
Temperatures		
Cloud cover		
Wind speed		
Rain		
Other features		

Fig 243 The characteristics of an anticyclone

Synoptic Charts

General weather conditions can be summarised on a synoptic chart like the ones in Fig 244. You should now be in a position to understand and explain the conditions shown on these charts, and to predict what the weather is going to be like in the next few hours.

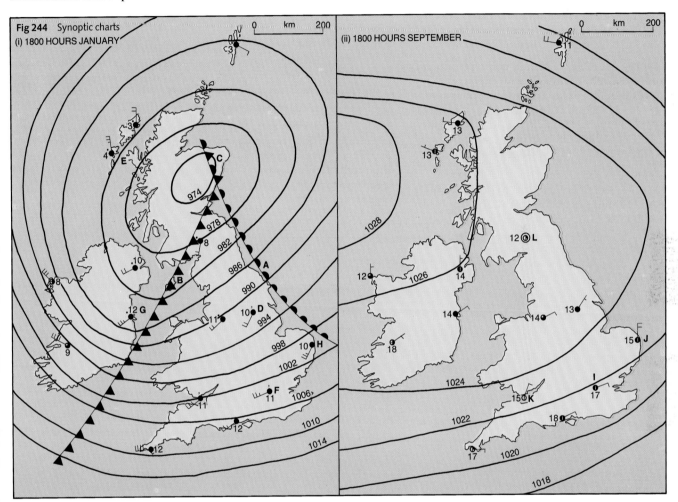

Fig 244 Synoptic charts
(i) 1800 HOURS JANUARY
(ii) 1800 HOURS SEPTEMBER

ENQUIRY

For Fig 244 (i)

1 What type of pressure system is shown? Name the fronts A, B and C.
2 Why is it warmer at D than E?
3 What type of cloud is most likely to be found at F, and G?
4 How would you describe wind speeds in southern England?
5 What are weather conditions at H likely to be by the morning?

For Fig 244 (ii)

6 What type of pressure system is shown?
7 Why is it warmer at I than J?
8 What type of cloud is most likely to be found at K?
9 How would you describe wind speeds in southern England?
10 What are weather conditions at L likely to be by the morning?

Why does it rain?

The basic cause of rain has already been referred to (see pages 98 and 104). As air rises it cools down and if temperatures fall below the condensation level (dew point) water vapour turns into water droplets which build up to form clouds.

However, for a cloud to rain other conditions have to be met. Firstly, for significant amounts of condensation to take place small particles of salt or dust (known as condensation nucleii) have to be present in the cloud in large numbers. This is because condensation takes place onto surfaces rather than just in the air.

Secondly, the droplets have to become heavy enough to fall out of the cloud. In temperate latitudes this is most likely to happen in the middle of a cloud where temperatures mean that there is a mixture of water droplets and ice crystals. Ice attracts water molecules and as a result the ice crystals quickly grow in size. Very often snowflakes form but they usually melt before they reach the ground. In tropical latitudes temperatures are too warm for ice crystals to form but the water droplets grow quickly as they collide with each other in strong air currents.

Strong air currents are also the cause of hailstones. These begin life as ordinary water droplets but they are repeatedly swept up to the top of a cloud where they pick up another layer of ice. When they become too heavy even for these air currents they fall out of the cloud.

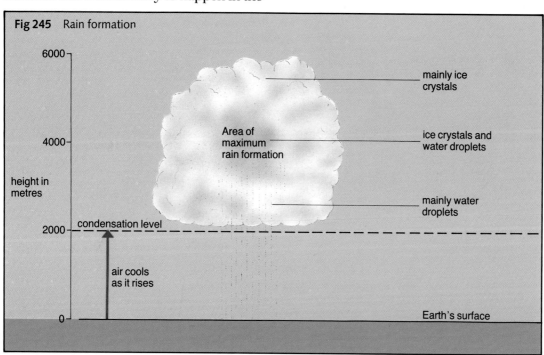

Fig 245 Rain formation

mainly ice crystals

Area of maximum rain formation

ice crystals and water droplets

height in metres

mainly water droplets

condensation level

air cools as it rises

Earth's surface

Types of rain

For rain to stand any chance of forming, a mass of air has to cool down. This is most likely to happen if the air is forced to rise. There are three main reasons why air is forced to rise and therefore there are three main types of rainfall.

1 Depression or Frontal rain   This happens because warm air is forced to rise at the fronts of a depression (Fig 246). Rain at the cold front is heavier than rain at the warm front because the air is forced to rise more quickly; the result is towering cumulonimbus clouds (see Fig 223, page 99).

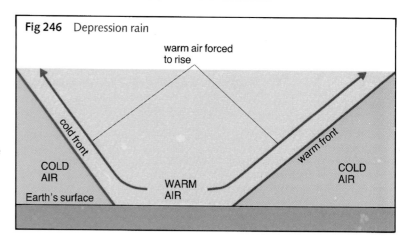

Fig 246 Depression rain

warm air forced to rise

cold front

warm front

COLD AIR

WARM AIR

COLD AIR

Earth's surface

2 Convection rain   This happens when air at the earth's surface is heated and therefore rises. As it rises it cools down, clouds form, and rain follows (Fig 247). Temperatures and relative humidity have to be high for this to happen. It is therefore common in equatorial regions, for example, but not in the hot deserts. Summer rain in the British Isles, when the weather is hot and humid, is often of this type.

The currents of rising air are strong. Consequently, water droplets have to reach a considerable size before they fall out of the cloud. This explains why convection rain tends to fall as heavy showers. Convection rain may occur as thunderstorms – in many parts of the tropics it is so hot and humid that a convectional thunderstorm happens nearly every afternoon.

3 Relief or Orographic rain   The third reason why air can be forced to rise is if it meets a chain of mountains (Fig 248). As it rises it cools down and the rain making process goes into operation. On the other side of the mountains the air falls. As it does so it warms up and the rain stops; this area is known as the rain shadow.

Cloud Seeding

There are many parts of the world which would benefit from a higher rainfall and for some 50 years there have been experiments to make clouds rain by adding artificial condensation nucleii. Early cloud seeding used dry ice (solid carbon dioxide). However, better results have been obtained with silver iodide but it is more expensive. In the USA millions of dollars have been spent on cloud seeding. Treated clouds do change form and do rain but our ability to predict the behaviour of clouds is limited . . . so what would have happened if the cloud hadn't been seeded?

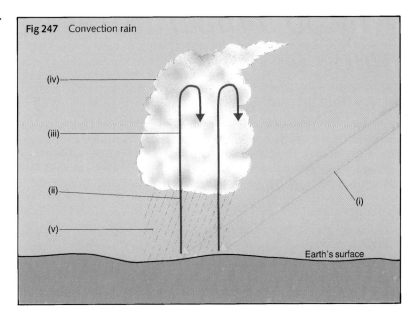

Fig 247   Convection rain

(iv)
(iii)
(ii)
(v)
(i)
Earth's surface

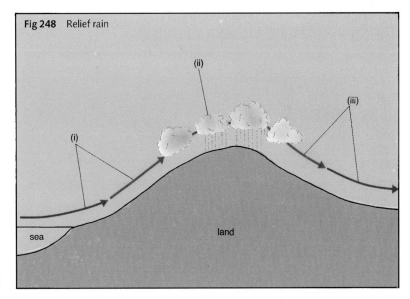

Fig 248   Relief rain

(ii)
(iii)
(i)
sea
land

1   What is the basic cause of rain?
2   Explain the role of condensation nucleii in the formation of rain.
3   Why is the size of a water droplet important to the formation of rain?
4   Why are there three different types of rain?
5   Explain why depressions are associated with rain.

6   Add labels to a copy of Fig 247 to explain how convection rain forms.
7   Add labels to a copy of Fig 248 to explain how relief rain forms.
8   Explain one way in which we could benefit from being able to change the weather and one way in which this ability could lead to problems.

Why do temperatures vary from place to place?

Energy from the Sun

With the exception of a small amount of heat from inside the earth, our heat comes from the sun's energy. However, only about 50% of the sun's energy – known as insolation – which enters the earth's atmosphere reaches the earth's surface. This is because approximately 20% is absorbed by the ozone layer and by water vapour, and 30% is reflected by clouds.

Solar insolation is in the form of short wave radiation which does very little heating as it passes through the atmosphere. However, it is absorbed by the earth's surface and is re-radiated in the form of long wave radiation which does heat up the atmosphere. The air is also heated by direct contact with the earth's surface (conduction) and by the movement of warm air currents (convection).

However, the energy budget shown in Fig 249 represents average conditions. Such conditions would produce uniform temperatures across the earth's surface but in reality we know that temperatures vary a great deal from place to place. In this Section the factors which influence these variations are examined.

ENQUIRY

1 Draw a pie graph to show the fate of solar insolation on entering the earth's atmosphere.
2 Explain the three main ways in which the atmosphere is heated.

Fig 249 The fate of solar insolation

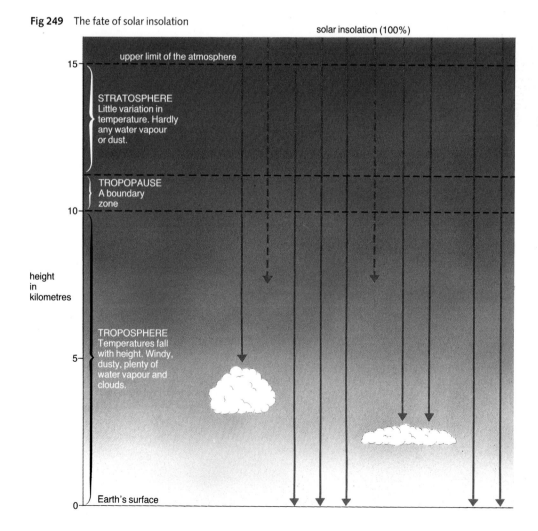

Latitude

In general, temperatures decrease as you move away from the equator. This is for two reasons. Firstly, the sun's rays are concentrated onto a smaller area of the earth's surface. Secondly, they have to travel a shorter distance through the atmosphere so there is less chance of being absorbed and/or reflected. These points are illustrated in Fig 250.

Altitude

As we have seen, the atmosphere is heated largely from the earth's surface. Water vapour and dust stop this heat from rapidly escaping back into space. However, as altitude increases, pressure decreases. A consequence of this is that the amount of water vapour and dust in the air also decreases and as a result heat is able to escape more rapidly. This explains why temperatures fall with altitude at an average rate of 6 °C per 1000 metres (Fig 251).

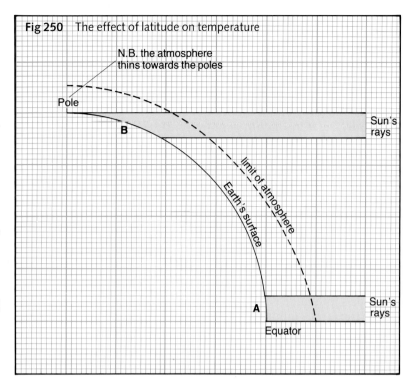

Fig 250   The effect of latitude on temperature

1   Compare the area the sun's rays are concentrated onto at the equator (A) and the pole (B) in Fig 250 by using the small squares as your unit of measurement. Compare the amount of atmosphere the sun's rays have to pass through at the two locations in the same way. Use your answers to explain why latitude affects temperature.

2   Explain why altitude affects temperature. If the surface temperature is 18 °C what is the temperature at a) 2000 metres and b) 3500 metres?

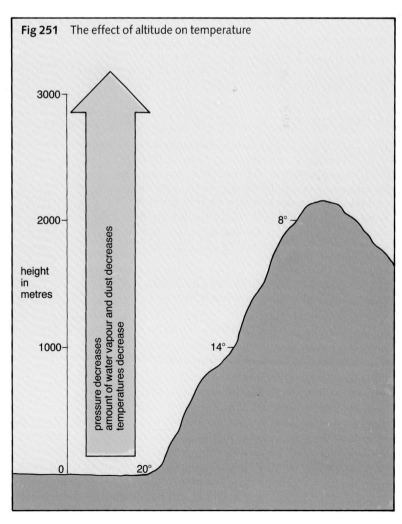

Fig 251   The effect of altitude on temperature

Distance from the Sea

The sea heats up more slowly than the land for two reasons. Firstly, water has a higher specific heat capacity. This means that it takes more solar insolation to heat up a particular amount of sea to the same temperature as an identical amount of land. Secondly, solar insolation penetrates the sea more deeply so its heating power is less concentrated than on land (Fig 252). Also, the sea cools down more slowly than the land because it loses heat by re-radiation more slowly.

Overall, therefore, the sea's temperature does not vary as much as the temperature of the land. This means that in the summer coastal areas are cooler than inland areas whereas in the winter they are warmer.

The sea's influence is described as maritime while the land's influence is described as continental. Winds blowing from the land to the sea soon pick up the land's influence so the contrast between maritime and continental climates is most noticeable when coastal regions are compared with the continental interiors (see the Enquiry on page 113). However, the beginnings of this effect can be seen soon after winds move inland (see the Enquiry on page 114).

Ocean Currents

There are three main causes of ocean currents. Most surface currents are caused by the prevailing winds. For example, the Gulf Stream is powered by strong north easterlies and reaches speeds of up to 220 km per day. Most of the water re-circulates back into the Gulf of Mexico in a clockwise direction but some of it veers off towards Europe as the North Atlantic Drift (Fig 253).

Convection currents are caused by warm water from the tropics flowing towards the poles; there it cools down, sinks, and returns to the tropics along the sea bed.

Differences in salinity (the saltiness of the sea) can also cause ocean currents. For example, water in the Mediterranean is saltier than water in the Atlantic because of the high rate of evaporation and the low rate of input from rain and rivers. An increase in salinity causes an increase in density and this, in turn, causes surface water to sink. As surface water in the Mediterranean sinks a current of less salty water is dragged in from the Atlantic through the Straits of Gibralter to take its place, and the process is repeated.

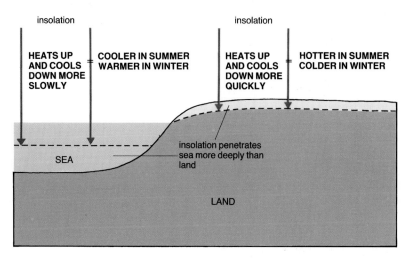

Fig 252   The effect of distance from the sea

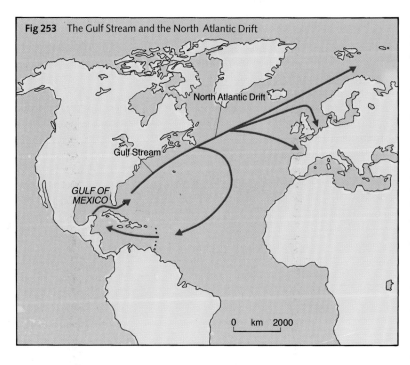

Fig 253   The Gulf Stream and the North Atlantic Drift

Ocean currents influence climate because they affect the temperature of winds blowing across them. The role of cold currents as a cause of deserts has already been considered (see page 81). In comparison, the North Atlantic Drift is a warm current and it brings mild, wet weather to the shores of Europe.

Other Factors

A range of other factors also affect temperature. Aspect means the direction in which a slope is facing. In the northern hemisphere the south facing slope gets the sun and is therefore warmer than the north facing slope which is in the shade. This influences landforms (see page 92) and land-use (Fig 254).

Clouds affect temperature because they cut down the amount of solar insolation reaching the earth, and because they keep in heat re-radiated by the earth. The clear skies of the hot deserts mean high temperatures during the day but low temperatures at night while on the equator the almost permanent layer of heavy cloud means that day time temperatures are lower than you might expect (typically 30 °C) but that night time temperatures fall only a little.

Length of day is another factor. Near the equator days and nights are the same length the whole year round and this helps to explain the low annual range of temperature in these regions. As you move away from the equator the seasonal variation in the length of day increases. The comparison between the short arctic summers when the sun never sets and the bitterly cold arctic winters when the sun never rises is a good example of this point.

ENQUIRY

1   Explain why distance from the sea affects temperature.
2   Use the information in an atlas about climatic regions to compare the annual range of temperature (the difference between the highest and lowest temperatures of the year) of a maritime region and the interior of a continental region. For example, you could compare Vancouver with Winnipeg in Canada, or Brest in France with Moscow in the USSR.
3   Explain the different causes of ocean currents.
4   What effect does the North Atlantic Drift have on the climate of north-western Europe?
5   How and why has aspect influenced land-use in Fig 254?
6   Briefly explain why cloud cover and length of day influence temperature.

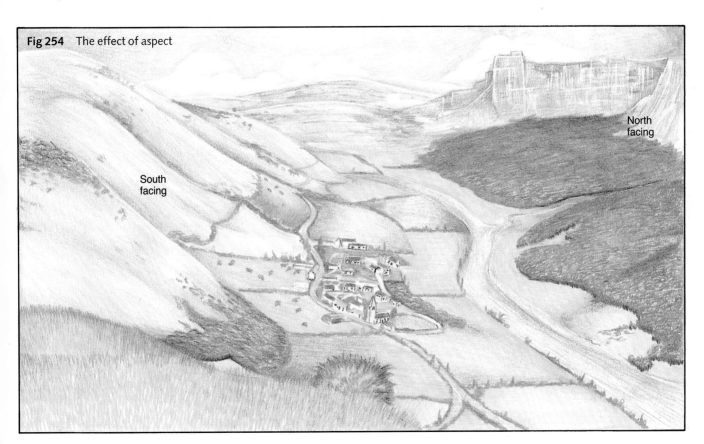

Fig 254 The effect of aspect

South facing

North facing

Explaining the Climate of the British Isles
– a Summary Exercise

(You will need an atlas with information about climate in the British Isles for this Enquiry.)

1 Make a copy of the four maps in Fig 255. Add the labels in the box to the correct half of each map. Add and label the North Atlantic Drift to Fig 255 (iv).

2 Use the information you have noted on these maps, any other information in the atlas such as climatic graphs and/or maps of prevailing winds, and information you have learnt in Sections 8.2 to 8.5 to complete the following tasks.

a) Describe the climate of the British Isles.

b) Explain the influence of the following factors on the climate of the British Isles – latitude; altitude and relief; distance from the sea (maritime and continental influences); and ocean currents.

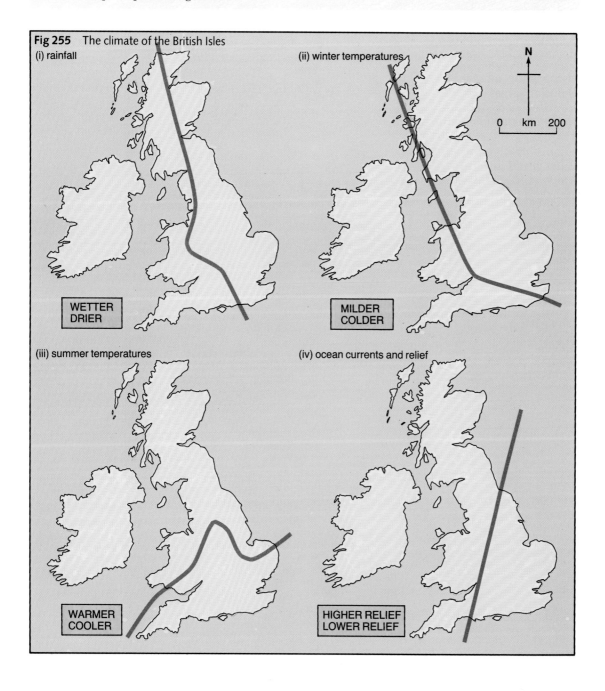

Fig 255 The climate of the British Isles

(i) rainfall

WETTER
DRIER

(ii) winter temperatures

MILDER
COLDER

(iii) summer temperatures

WARMER
COOLER

(iv) ocean currents and relief

HIGHER RELIEF
LOWER RELIEF

What is a microclimate?

The climate of the British Isles is described by meteorologists as "cool temperate western marginal". This type of climate is characterised by average monthly winter temperatures of between 2° C and 7° C, average monthly summer temperatures of between 13° C and 15° C, and an evenly distributed total annual rainfall of about 750 mm. However, these general conditions vary a great deal from place to place, even over short distances and microclimate is the term used to describe these local variations.

A range of factors affect the microclimate of a particular area. The main ones are soils, relief, vegetation, water, snow and ice, and the urban environment.

Soils

Different types of soil have different albedos (Fig 256). (Albedo is the percentage of solar insolation reflected by a particular surface.) Lighter soils have a higher albedo and therefore reflect more solar insolation than darker soils. As a result, lighter soils re-radiate less energy which, in turn, means lower ground temperatures (Fig 257). Wetter soils have a lower albedo and are therefore associated with higher temperatures.

Relief

The effects of aspect on temperature (page 113) and relief on rainfall (page 109) have already been discussed. However, there are other ways in which relief affects climate. For example, soft fruit such as strawberries can be grown in the Carse of Gowrie and the Vale of Strathmore in Scotland despite their northerly latitude because they are protected from cold winds by the southern flanks of the Grampian Highlands and the Sidlaw Hills (Fig 258).

Fig 256 Soil albedo

SOIL	ALBEDO	
	DRY	WET
black – brown clay soil	14%	8%
yellow sandy soil	20%	10%

Fig 257   The effect of soil albedo

(i) lighter soil

less re-radiation means lower temperatures

more insolation is reflected

(ii) darker soil

less insolation is reflected

more re-radiation means higher temperatures

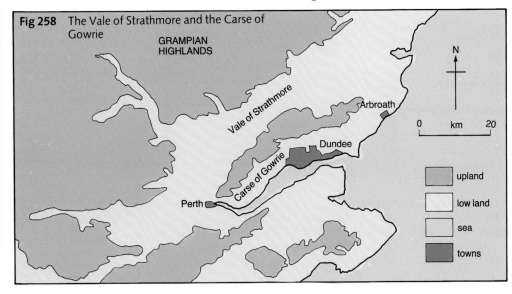

Fig 258   The Vale of Strathmore and the Carse of Gowrie

GRAMPIAN HIGHLANDS

N

Vale of Strathmore

Arbroath

Carse of Gowrie

Dundee

Perth

0   km   20

upland
low land
sea
towns

Vegetation

Even short grass affects temperature because firstly, it prevents solar insolation from reaching the soil by reflecting and absorbing it and secondly, it traps energy which is re-radiated by the soil. As a result, vegetated surfaces have lower temperatures than sur-rounding areas of bare soil during the day but warmer temperatures at night time.

The forest microclimate is particularly dis-tinctive (Fig 259). Forest albedos typically range between 10% and 20%. This means that the forest floor is 0.6° C cooler, on average, in comparison with open country. However, it is cooler than this during the day while at night time it is actually warmer than the surrounding countryside. Forests also reduce wind speed. Experiments in Euro-pean forests have shown that 60 metres into a forest wind speeds are cut by 50% and that 120 metres into a forest wind speeds are cut by over 90%. Interception of rainfall is another significant factor. Interception rates vary according to the type of tree, whether or not it is in leaf and the characteristics of the rainfall; for example, a pine forest can inter-cept over 90% of drizzle but only 15% of heavy rain.

Fig 259 The forest microclimate

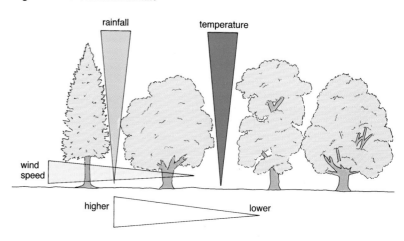

Water

The moderating influence of the sea has already been discussed (page 112). However, large bodies of water affect the climate in other ways as well. For example, the air is likely to have a greater relative humidity and precipitation tends to be higher in coastal districts.

On a hot day the sea can also influence wind (Fig 260). During the day time the land heats up more quickly than the sea. Low pressure develops over the land and high pressure develops over the sea. As a result, an onshore breeze begins to blow. At night time the situation is reversed. However, these differ-ences in pressure are very localised; inland, the prevailing wind is unaffected.

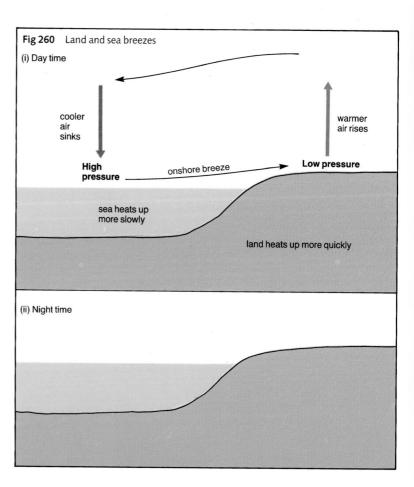

Fig 260 Land and sea breezes

(i) Day time

cooler air sinks

warmer air rises

High pressure ── onshore breeze ──→ **Low pressure**

sea heats up more slowly

land heats up more quickly

(ii) Night time

Snow and Ice

White surfaces have a very high albedo. Snow, for example, reflects about 90% of solar insolation. Therefore, the presence of snow and ice is not only associated with cold temperatures but it further reduces ground temperatures. This has been suggested as one of the mechanisms involved in the causes of an Ice Age i.e. once an ice sheet has built up it cools temperatures still further which causes more ice to build up, and so on.

The Urban Environment

The building of towns and cities has created a unique microclimate. Average annual temperatures are between 0.5° C and 1° C higher than in the surrounding countryside because tarmac, concrete and brick have low albedos and because there is an input of heat from fires and car exhausts etc. This is known as the "heat island" effect and the contrast is greatest at night when buildings release the insolation they have absorbed during the day.

Pollution from fires and exhausts etc has a series of effects. The number of particles which could act as condensation nucleii has been found to be up to 10 times as great in urban areas. This could help to explain the higher rainfall totals which have been recorded in towns and cities. The "heat island" effect which encourages convection currents to develop is probably important to this explanation as well.

Pollution by gases from the burning of fossil fuels, such as coal and oil, and from industry affects visibility. For example, the photo-chemical smogs of Los Angeles (Fig 261) are the result of complex chemical reactions involving the more than 12 000 tons of pollutants produced by the city each day. Particles

Fig 261
Photochemical smog

and gases are unable to escape because Los Angeles is surrounded by hills on three sides and has very stable air.

Cloud cover is 5% to 10% greater in urban areas because of pollution and the amount of sunshine is correspondingly lower. The incidence of fog in the winter is 100% greater in urban areas.

Buildings break up the wind and reduce overall wind speeds by 20% to 30%. However, tall buildings can funnel winds along "wind corridors" at very high speeds. Wind corridors can be inconvenient and dangerous and architects are now required to consider the effect their buildings have on airflow.

Condition	Increase in Temperature	Decrease in Temperature
lighter coloured soils compared with darker coloured soils		
southerly aspect compared with northerly aspect		
grass compared with bare soil		
snow covered ground compared with waterlogged ground		

Fig 262   Some factors affecting microclimates

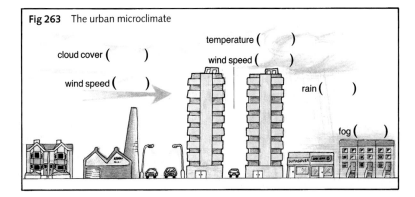

Fig 263   The urban microclimate

cloud cover (   )

temperature (   )

wind speed (   )

wind speed (   )

rain (   )

fog (   )

WEATHER SURVEYS

The weather offers many opportunities for collecting simple but useful data. The ideas listed here are only a few examples of what you could do. They are included in this Section about microclimate because in most cases that is what you will be recording.

TEMPERATURE SURVEY

Aim   To study the effect of aspect on temperature.

Equipment   Thermometer.

Method   Compare temperatures on the south and north facing sides of a house at different times during the day.

Alternative   If you were able to borrow two Six's thermometers you could position one on the south and one on the north facing side of a house and compare maximum and minimum temperatures.

WIND SPEED AND DIRECTION SURVEY

Aim   To test the idea that wind speed and direction are affected by the urban environment.

Equipment   Compass. Ideally a hand-held anemometer but you could use the Beaufort Wind Scale instead.

Method   Choose a route across a town which preferably starts in the surrounding countryside (Fig 264). At 100 metre intervals (pace this) record wind speed and direction and make a note of the surroundings e.g. fields, tall buildings, narrow streets, etc.

RAIN SURVEY

Aim   To examine variations in rainfall in a back garden.

Equipment   Three or four rain gauges would be ideal for this experiment. However, you could improvise with tins, as long as they have the same diameter, and a graduated test tube. Your "units of rain" will then be consistent although they will not be comparable with meteorological statistics.

Method   Place the rain gauges in different parts of the garden e.g. near the house, in the middle of the lawn, next to the back fence. Take daily measurements of rainfall. Note also the direction the rain came from.

WEATHER FOR A WEEK SURVEY

You can complete a record sheet like the one in Fig 265 without any equipment at all, as long as you know in which direction north is! Choose the same place and time each day to make your results more comparable. Your finished table will be interesting in its own right but try to collect synoptic charts from a newspaper because you will then be able to explain the weather you have observed.

This table could be easily added to. For example, if you could borrow a hygrometer and a barometer you could record relative humidity and air pressure. You could then relate these measurements to the prevailing weather conditions.

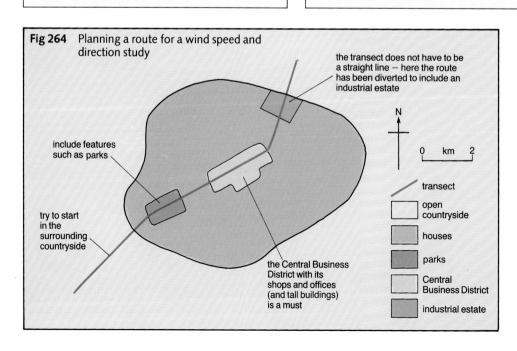

Fig 264   Planning a route for a wind speed and direction study

the transect does not have to be a straight line — here the route has been diverted to include an industrial estate

include features such as parks

try to start in the surrounding countryside

the Central Business District with its shops and offices (and tall buildings) is a must

N

0   km   2

transect

open countryside

houses

parks

Central Business District

industrial estate

Day Date Time	Temperature (describe)	Precipitation (state if raining etc.)	Wind direction	Wind (on the Beaufort Wind Scale)	Cloud cover	Cloud type	Any other comments
Sunday 7/8/88 12.20 pm	hot	—	S.W.	2	◐	cirro-stratus	a lovely day!

Fig 265   A week's weather observations

Weather and people

The weather affects our lives in so many ways that it would be impossible to list them all; some examples are given in Fig 266. The weather can even lead to political controversy, as you can see from Fig 267.

Keep a page in your exercise book or folder for newspaper cuttings about the weather. It should not be long before you fill it up!

Fig 266   The weather

(i)

(ii)

(iii)

(iv)

(v)

Severe weather pay blocked by new test

By Peter Hildrew and Susan Tirbutt

More than half of the severe weather payments made last winter would have been disallowed under present rules, the Society of Civil and Public Servants alleged yesterday.

Social security offices are now linked in groups to 64 weather stations, and cold weather payments can only be made if the station temperature averages minus 1.5 degrees Celsius for a week measured from Monday to Sunday.

More than 220,000 of the 412,000 payments to benefit claimants made this year would have failed this test, according to comparisons of internal figures carried out by the union.

Large areas of London, North-east England and Scotland would have failed to qualify, despite the very severe cold snap last February. Fewer than 10,000 claimants would have received four weeks' payments, and the total cost to the Government would have been £1.76 million compared with more than £4 million believed to have been spent.

"The figures show that a change in a system badly needing simplification has been used to hide a massive cut," said Mr Graham Hodkinson, assistant secretary of the union's DHSS staff group.

The temperature figures may even underestimate the cut, because the new regulations have also narrowed the categories of people on supplementary benefit who can claim the payments to help with their heating costs. Only households containing someone aged over 65, someone chronically sick or disabled, or a child aged under two, can apply.

A spokeswoman for Age Concern said that the temperature threshold for the new scheme had been set too low. Ministers have justified the scheme, however, on the basis that exceptionally severe cold weather should not be deemed to have occurred more often than once in five years on average.

Government plans to outlaw leasing arrangements used by local councils to install central heating for pensioners and other tenants have had to be dropped because of the political sensitivity of anti-hypothermia campaigns.

● Age Concern's director, Mr David Hobman, has protested to the Social Services Secretary, Mr Norman Fowler, over plans to cut heating assistance to 90,000 supplementary benefit claimants when the new income support system takes effect in 1988.

Fig 267   Cold weather payments

ENVIRONMENTAL ISSUES

Deforestation

Deforestation means clearing trees. Vast areas of forest in Europe and North America have been cleared in the past to make way for farming and settlement. There is very little of Britain's original forest left. Most 'natural' landscapes are man-made – for example, the windswept hills in Fig 268 were once wooded.

Deforestation is still taking place in More Developed Countries (MDCs). For example, 50% of our ancient woodland has been cleared in the last 40 years. However, deforestation is more of an issue in Less Developed Countries (LDCs) because the rate of clearance is so great – for example, 7% of the tropical rain forest (Fig 269) is cleared every year which is equivalent to an area the size of Britain.

Clearing the Tropical Rain Forest

There are three main reasons for this clearance –

- to provide farmland for settlers. For example, there are more than 2.5 million landless people in Brasil and one solution has been to clear land in the Amazon rain forest for smallholdings.

- to provide land for cattle ranches. For example, two thirds of the Central American rain forest has been cleared since 1950 to make way for beef cattle. Nearly all of the

Fig 268   The Northumbrian Dales

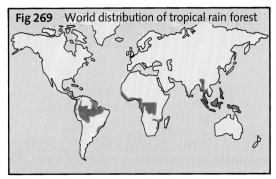

Fig 269   World distribution of tropical rain forest

land is bought by multinational companies or rich landowners and nearly all of the meat is exported to make hamburgers in MDCs.

- to exploit valuable timber reserves. Timber exports earn LDCs about $8.7 billion dollars a year. Hardwoods such as teak and mahogany are particularly valuable. LDCs need export earnings for many reasons including the repayment of loans and debts.

Fig 270   The tropical rain forest

Fig 271   Tropical deforestation

ENVIRONMENTAL ISSUES

However, clearing the tropical rain forest presents a number of serious problems. Firstly, the lush tropical vegetation suggests a rich soil but this is not the case (Fig 272). The rain forest ecosystem survives by storing most of its nutrients in the trees and plants themselves. When a tree dies it quickly decomposes in the hot, humid conditions and the nutrients which are released are almost immediately taken up by the shallow roots of living trees and plants. When the forest is cleared this cycle is broken. Any nutrients in the soil are quickly washed away. This leaves the land infertile, liable to erosion and useless for farming.

It is interesting to note that the traditional farming system of these areas – slash and burn – had adapted to these conditions. An area of forest was cleared by cutting and burning. Large tree stumps were left in and this gave the soil some protection. The ash from the burning provided nutrients. After a few years when the fertility of the soil began to fall the clearing was abandoned and a new one made. However, this type of land-use can only support a low population density.

Secondly, nearly half the world's animals and plants live in the tropical forest and the present rate of clearance means that two species become extinct every hour. An enormous genetic pool is being lost to science. Its value is easy to demonstrate – many of our medicines came originally from the tropical forest and only recently scientists were able to develop a drug to fight leukemia from a rare tropical plant, the rosy periwinkle.

Thirdly, clearing the forest breaks the carbon cycle and increases the amount of carbon dioxide in the atmosphere. This contributes towards the Greenhouse Effect (see pages 125 to 126) and could therefore have global consequences.

Fig 272 Soil fertility in the tropics

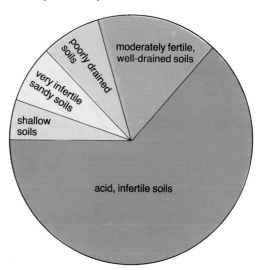

Fourthly, forest clearance upsets the hydrological cycle. The forest acts like a giant sponge by intercepting and storing rainfall. When it is cleared surface runoff increases dramatically. This can lead to flooding as has already happened, for example, in Bangladesh.

Another example of deforestation upsetting the hydrological cycle is the threat faced by the Panama Canal (Fig 273). The canal system is fed by water from Gatun Lake. In the four month dry season the lake is kept full by water seeping out from the tropical forest. However, deforestation is increasing surface runoff in the wet season and reducing the catchment area's ability to act as a reservoir for the dry season. The water is also bringing more silt with it. Unless this issue is tackled the canal, which is very important to international trade and vital to the Panamanian economy, could run out of water for at least part of the year.

ENQUIRY

1   What is deforestation?
2   Re-draw Fig 268 to show a 'natural' landscape!
3   Why is the tropical forest being cleared?
4   What is the main disadvantage of slash and burn agriculture?
5   Explain why tropical deforestation is a problem.
6   How could the following suggestions reduce tropical deforestation – stop eating hamburgers; use recycled paper; write off LDCs' debts.
7   We have already cleared our forests. Do we have any right to tell LDCs not to clear theirs?

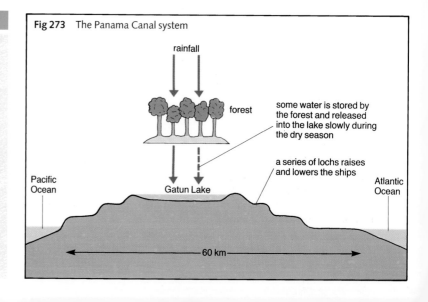

Fig 273   The Panama Canal system

Desertification

Desertification is the process by which land becomes desert. This is happening on the margins of a number of the world's hot deserts – notably the Californian, Atacama, Sahara, Kalahari and Thar deserts – with a total of 15 million acres a year being affected.

However, the problem is greatest in the Sahel, a belt of land to the south of the Sahara, where the desert is advancing in places at the rate of 6 kilometres every year (Fig 274).

Desertification in the Sahel

In 1984–85 30 million Africans were affected by drought. Most of them lived in the Sahel and the terrible consequences of drought and desertification have rarely been out of the news in recent years (Fig 275). There has been a massive international relief effort but the problem remains. Is desertification the inevitable result of climatic change or is it a problem we could solve?

The causes of desertification are complex and far from clear. There is some evidence of a change towards a drier climate in the Sahel. Statistics show that average annual rainfall has decreased since 1950. This has been linked to an increase in rainfall in temperate latitudes and it has been suggested that these changes are the result of global shifts in atmospheric circulation, perhaps because of the Greenhouse Effect (see pages 125 to 126). However, even if this change is permanent, it alone is unable to explain the relentless and rapid march of the deserts.

Population pressure has almost certainly played its part. The traditional farming systems of the Sahel are slash and burn and nomadic grazing. Both these systems give the land time to recover before it is used again but they can support only low population densities.

In the last 30 years population growth rates in the countries of the Sahel have been high and this has placed an extra pressure on the land. Fields have been given shorter rest periods and soil fertility and structure have suffered as a result; this, in turn, has caused lower crop yields and soil erosion. The number of livestock has been increased and this has led to overgrazing; this, in turn, means that the soil has lost its protective covering of vegetation and is liable to erosion.

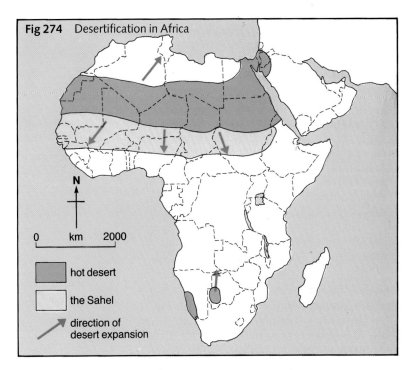

Fig 274 Desertification in Africa

hot desert

the Sahel

direction of desert expansion

Fig 275 Drought in the Sahel

A larger population has meant an increase in the demand for wood for fuel which has led to deforestation. This also leaves the soil unprotected, and the resource a farming community depends on is blown or washed away.

Changes in farming practices may also have contributed to the process of desertification. Settled agriculture with an emphasis on cash crops has been encouraged by many countries as a strategy for rural development. However, this already fragile environment requires very careful management if it is to be farmed intensively or problems of soil exhaustion soon set in.

The climate of the Sahel has changed in the past and there is evidence of the Sahara being both larger and smaller than it is at the present time. However, it is clear that our activities are at least partly, if not wholly, to blame for the present rate of desertification and it should therefore be possible to take some actions to make the situation better – especially when you consider the achievements irrigation schemes in the real desert have made, such as the ones discussed in Section 6.

However, the countries of the Sahel are poor and the majority of the people are subsistence farmers. Perhaps not surprisingly small-scale, inexpensive schemes which increase food production in a short period of time have been the most popular and the most successful ways of tackling the problem.

Reafforestation has taken place, wells have been drilled and small dams have been built. More recently, the use of 'magic stones' has been developed (Fig 277). These are simply lines of stones running parallel to the contours of the land. They hold back rainfall which would normally run straight off the hard tropical surface, and give it time to sink in. The result is crop yields up by an average of 50%! Stones are in plentiful supply and the only equipment needed is a simple level to get a correct alignment with the contours – Oxfam have developed one which costs a mere £3.50 to make.

Nevertheless, the problem of desertification remains a very serious one and a great deal more needs to be done if this threat is to be significantly reduced.

ENQUIRY

1 What is desertification?
2 Use an atlas to help you name the countries which make up the Sahel in Africa.
3 Add labels to a copy of Fig 276 to complete an explanation of the possible causes of desertification. In particular, add extra arrows if you think factors are interrelated.
4 Draw a diagram to explain how 'magic stones' work.

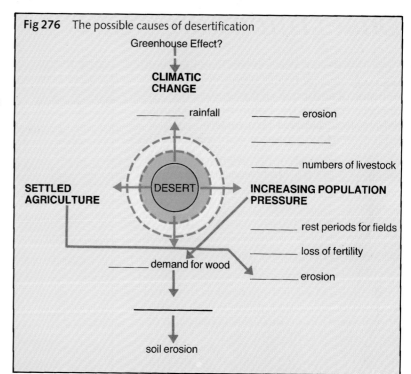

Fig 276   The possible causes of desertification

Greenhouse Effect?

CLIMATIC CHANGE

_____ rainfall   _____ erosion

_____

_____ numbers of livestock

SETTLED AGRICULTURE   DESERT   INCREASING POPULATION PRESSURE

_____ rest periods for fields

_____ loss of fertility

_____ demand for wood   _____ erosion

_____

soil erosion

Fig 277   Magic stones

The Greenhouse Effect

The Greenhouse Effect is the name given to the process which could cause global temperatures to rise because of increasing amounts of gases in the atmosphere which trap heat re-radiated by the earth (Fig 278).

The most important 'Greenhouse gas' is carbon dioxide (CO_2). 18 billion tonnes is released into the atmosphere each year mainly through the burning of fossil fuels – coal, oil and natural gas – and wood.

Until recently, the carbon cycle enabled the earth to maintain a steady amount of CO_2 in the atmosphere (Fig 279). Animal life breathes in oxygen and breathes out CO_2. Half of this CO_2 dissolves in the top layers of the oceans and supports life like plankton. The other half is absorbed by plants and converted into vegetable tissue. This traps the carbon but releases the oxygen, allowing it to go through the cycle again. When the plants die and decay some of the CO_2 is released back into the atmosphere while the rest is stored e.g. in coal.

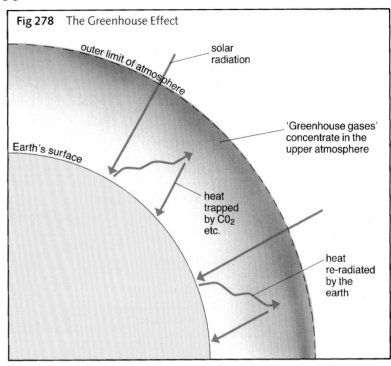

Fig 278   The Greenhouse Effect

outer limit of atmosphere

solar radiation

'Greenhouse gases' concentrate in the upper atmosphere

Earth's surface

heat trapped by CO_2 etc.

heat re-radiated by the earth

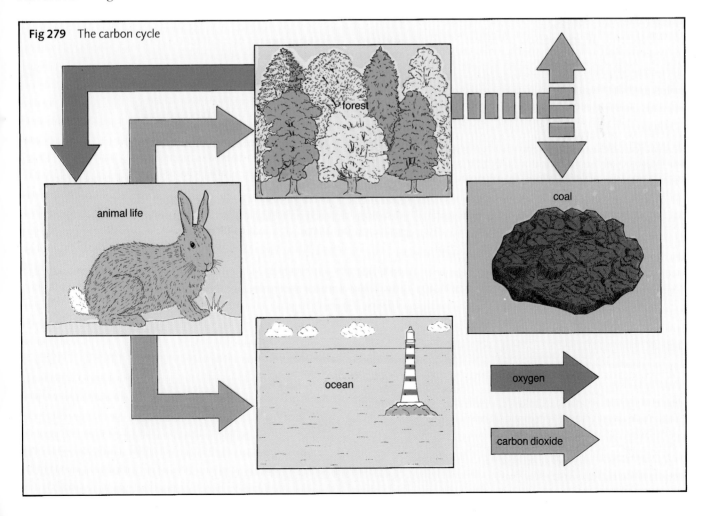

Fig 279   The carbon cycle

forest

animal life

coal

ocean

oxygen

carbon dioxide

This cycle has now been upset. Figure 280 shows the increase in CO_2 in the atmosphere since 1958 and its predicted level by 2050.

CO_2 is not the only 'Greenhouse gas'. Atmospheric levels of chlorofluorocarbons (CFCs) which are used in aerosol sprays and foam packaging are increasing by 5% a year and these add to the Greenhouse Effect. (CFCs also damage the ozone layer in the stratosphere. It protects us from harmful ultraviolet radiation which, among other things, can cause skin cancer.) Methane from cattle manure, and nitrogen oxides from car engines and boilers also add to the level of 'Greenhouse gases'.

What are the Likely Consequences of the Greenhouse Effect?

The Greenhouse Effect means warmer global temperatures; there is already evidence that temperatures have risen by 0.5°C since 1900. However, regional effects are very difficult to predict, simply because we do not yet know enough about how the weather system works. Wind belts and ocean currents would shift, and with them the rain belts. Some places would benefit but others would become hotter and drier – desertification could become an increasing problem.

Global warming would be uneven. The greatest increase in temperature would be at the poles and this would cause the ice sheets to melt. As a result, sea-levels would rise. The '2050' prediction would produce an increase in sea-level of between 0.5 to 1.5 metres. This has major consequences for low-lying areas the world over but particularly in LDCs which are less able to afford flood protection schemes.

An increase in CO_2 would cause overall plant growth to increase but some plants respond to CO_2 more than others. Experiments have shown that weeds which grow alongside subsistence crops in LDCs such as maize and sorghum unfortunately do much better than the crops.

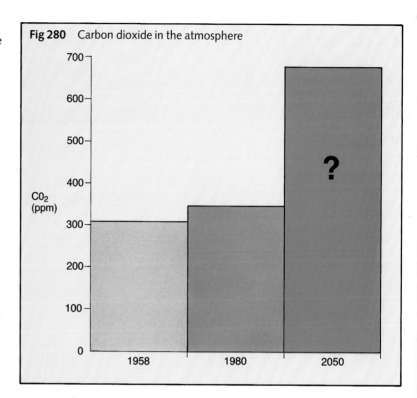

Fig 280   Carbon dioxide in the atmosphere

Can Anything be Done?

Conventional power stations are a major source of CO_2. They could be replaced with nuclear power stations but these bring with them their own problems which many people, and an increasing number of governments, find unacceptable. Forests could be planted to absorb the CO_2 but it has been estimated that 250 000 acres of trees are needed to counteract the effects from an average power station and this seems unrealistic at a time when the world's forests are being destroyed at an increasing rate. Some gases for which alternatives could be developed, such as CFCs, could be banned. A more efficient use of fossil fuels e.g. better engines, and filters on power stations could stop the amount of CO_2 from rising above 60% of its '2050' level. Above all, everyone must see that the Greenhouse Effect is a real threat.

ENQUIRY

1 Design a large poster to explain what is meant by the Greenhouse Effect and why we should all take it seriously. Include its causes, its consequences and what we can do about it ... but remember, you are trying to change people's attitudes so keep the message simple, accurate and effective.

INDEX